WHITAKER'S
WORLD OF
WEIRD

Pembroke Branch Tel. 6689575

A & C Black • London

Published 2008 by
A & C Black Publishers Ltd.
38 Soho Square, London, W1D 3HB
www.acblack.com

ISBN 978-1-4081-0453-8

Text copyright © 2008 Tracey Turner

The right of Tracey Turner to be identified
as the author of this work has been
asserted by her in accordance with the
Copyrights, Designs and Patents Act 1988.

A CIP catalogue for this book is available
from the British Library.

This book is produced using paper that is
made from wood grown in managed,
sustainable forests. It is natural,
renewable and recyclable. The logging
and manufacturing processes conform to
the environmental regulations of the
country of origin.

Design and illustration by Splinter Group.
Cover illustration by KJA-artists.com.
Printed and bound in China by Leo Paper
Products.

Every effort has been made to contact
copyright holders of material reproduced
in this book. Any omissions will be
rectified in subsequent printings if notice
is given to the publishers.

Contents

WEIRD LIFE

WEIRD EARTH

WEIRD ENCOUNTERS

Introduction

Have you ever noticed anything a little... weird? Maybe you've encountered a series of strange coincidences, or seen an Unidentified Flying Object. Perhaps you've witnessed the mysterious sliding rocks of Death Valley, or taken up bog snorkelling. Whether you've had weird experiences of your own or not, you're about to find out that the world is full of weirdness.

In the natural world, there's the beetle with the toxic bottom, a Colossal squid, and bizarre rains of fish, frogs and worms. Then there are the weird things made by people: a huge chandelier made from human bones, a machine that can see through solid walls, and a giant duck-shaped building. And there's a whole world of unexplained mysteries and monsters...

- Meet some strange and terrifying creatures: a brain-sucking ape, the Beast of Bodmin Moor, vampires and zombies.
- Find out about man-eating trees and strange lights in the sky.
- Investigate ghosts, out-of-body-experiences, ESP, and the eerie feeling of déjà vu.

As well as hundreds of amazing facts and figures about the world's weirdest phenomena, this book also includes weird things to do. Discover how to make your own ectoplasm, bring a dead plant back to life, and even how to levitate.

Read on, and find out answers to the weird questions on everyone's lips...

- Is it really possible to read minds?
- What is exploding head syndrome?
- How do crop circles appear?
- Where can I find a collection of 3,000 human brains?

At the bottom

The deepest part of the sea is 11,000 m (36,000 ft) below the surface. At only 1,000 m (3,300 ft) down it's freezing cold, almost completely dark and the pressure of the water above would squish you instantly. But there are plenty of bizarre creatures who can survive down there...

Fangtooths have been given their name because of the two long fangs on their lower jaw. These scary fangs mean they are also sometimes called 'ogrefish'. The teeth are so long that they slide into special pockets either side of the fish's brain, to avoid puncturing it. Relative to its size, the fangtooth has the largest teeth of any fish in the ocean – thankfully, the fangtooth doesn't grow much bigger than 15 cm (6 in) long.

The deep sea anglerfish: one of the ugliest creatures on earth.

The deep sea anglerfish lurks menacingly at depths of up to 2,000 m (6,500 ft). The fish has a long, fleshy growth sprouting from its head, with a shining bulb on the end, which it dangles in front of its cavernous mouth. This cunning trick is a way of luring its prey within biting distance. When it is in reach, the fish can engulf a creature that is even bigger than itself, thanks to its huge mouth and elastic stomach.

Many strange creatures roam the deep oceans but we know very little about them – there hasn't been much exploration of the sea bed. There are almost certainly dozens of deep sea species waiting to be discovered. Two recent discoveries are the Megamouth Shark and the Colossal Squid. In 2007, fishermen caught a 10-m- (30-ft-) long Colossal Squid, the largest example so far.

TOXIC CREATURES

There are thousands of different toxic creatures in the world, many of them dangerous to people. Poisonous animals have poison in or on their bodies that is passed on if they are touched or eaten, while venomous creatures inject poison by biting or stinging. Both are best avoided!

Deadly jellies

The most venomous animal on earth lives in the sea: it is the box jellyfish. The largest species of box jellyfish has about 60 stinging tentacles, each up to 3 m (10 ft) long. These tentacles can sting even if they are detached from the animal's body, or after the jellyfish has died. The box jellyfish has 24 eyes and can propel itself through the water at up to 2 m (7 ft) per second. The pain of its sting is so terrible that victims often go into shock and drown. A box jellyfish's body contains enough venom to kill 60 adults.

The blue-ringed octopus is only the size of a golfball when fully grown, yet its bite can kill a person in minutes.

Another species of box jellyfish has been known to kill people – despite not being much bigger than your thumbnail.

The world's most poisonous creature...

...is a beautiful tree frog that lives in the South American rainforest. The golden poison frog only contains about a milligram of poison, yet that small amount could kill up to 20 adult humans. Local people sometimes coat their arrowheads with poison from the frogs to make them extra deadly for hunting. But the golden poison frog has a secret: it loses its poison when it is taken away from its natural habitat. Could it be that the world's most poisonous creature is not the golden poison frog at all but a tiny insect that the frogs feed on?

www.animalcorner.com/venanimals/ven_about.html

Sea creatures

Life in the sea began more than 3 billion years ago, over 2.5 billion years before any animals evolved on the land. The ocean covers 362 million square km (225 million square miles) – that's over 70% of Earth's surface. If you think about these amazing facts, it's no surprise that the sea is home to some of the weirdest creatures on the planet.

Slippery customers

Hagfish are incredibly slimy. In order to escape predators, the eel-like sea creatures produce a sticky mucus from their skin which makes them difficult to catch. Their slimy skin also lets them slip right inside the bodies of the dead and dying fish they feed on. Hagfish are the only fish that can sneeze, which helps clear the slime from their single nostril. They clear the slimy mucus from their skin by tying themselves in a knot.

Tight squeeze

Members of the cephalopod family, which includes octopus and squid, have three hearts, their blood is blue and they can change shape – which, you have to admit, is pretty weird. An octopus doesn't have a skeleton, so it can squeeze through tiny gaps: a 30-kg (66-lb) octopus in an American lab escaped through a hole just 10 cm (4 in) wide.

Regeneration

Starfish can grow new arms if they lose any in a nasty accident. It's possible for a completely new starfish to grow from a single arm if it is attached to just a small part of the centre of the starfish body. Starfish also have a weird way of eating: they can eject one of their two stomachs from their bodies to engulf and digest prey (shellfish is their favourite meal). The stomach then slips back inside the starfish, leaving behind nothing but the empty shell of their victim.

The strange violet sea snail spends most of its life hanging upside down from a floating raft of slime bubbles.

Creepy crawlies

Most insects, spiders, worms and other creepy crawlies look pretty weird to us, probably because they're so different from human beings. The number of creepy crawlies on Earth is hard to imagine – there are over a million different species, and that's just the ones that have been named. That's an awful lot of scuttling, slithering, many-legged mini-monsters. Here are some of the weirdest...

Giant gurgling worms

If you're ever wandering about and hear strange gurglings coming from beneath your feet, it could be an enormous earthworm. The giant Gippsland earthworms are found in Australia and they have been known to grow up to 4 m (13 ft) long. They're known as 'gurgling worms' because when they hear noises above ground they ooze liquid from their bodies, making strange burps and bubbling sounds.

Caterpillar poo

Predators of the Skipper Caterpillar are attracted by the
chemicals in the creature's faeces which help them to
track it down. But the caterpillar has managed to
get one step ahead. It fools predators by
keeping as far away from its own waste as
possible: it fires its poo long distances –
up to 40 times its own body length.

Exploding beetles

The Bombardier Beetle has an extraordinary
ability: it can blast toxic steam from its rear end. The
beetle stores two different chemicals in separate parts of its
body. When it is threatened by a predator, the beetle squirts the
chemicals into a thick-walled internal chamber, where a
chemical reaction takes place. The reaction makes the
beetle spray out a blast of poisonous steam, along with
a loud popping noise for added effect. Scientists have
studied the beetle's amazing defence mechanism to
develop new kinds of fuel injection systems and
fire extinguishers.

Bizarre birds and remarkable reptiles

One of the strangest looking birds in the world is the huge Southern Cassowary bird of the Australian rainforest. Cassowaries grow up to 2 m (7 ft) tall, they can run at 50 km/h (30 mph) and jump to a height of 1.5 m (5 ft) but the Cassowary can't fly! People don't often get a chance to see the birds because they tend to be very shy. Perhaps that's just as well: the Cassowary has three sharp claws on each foot. The middle claw is 12 cm (5 in) long and capable of disembowelling an enemy with a strong kick.

Frigatebirds are sea birds that catch fish and scavenge for food, sometimes stealing from other birds. Another of their tactics for finding food is to attack birds in mid-flight and force them to regurgitate their last meal. The frigatebird swoops below to catch the other bird's vomit in mid-air and eat it.

Komodo dragons are huge, 3-m (10-ft) lizards. They can eat up to 80% of their own body weight in one meal – that's more than 55 kg (120 lbs)! They kill prey with a combination of mild venom and millions of deadly bacteria in their saliva. Even though the bacteria will kill most animals, the komodo dragon is immune to it. Scientists are trying to discover the komodo dragon's secret, in the hope of finding an antibacterial medicine.

Horned Lizards have an unusual way of scaring off unwanted visitors. As well as keeping themselves camouflaged, they can puff up their bodies and make their spiny scales stand on end. They can even squirt blood from their eyeballs – giving predators a bit of a shock!

Weird mammals

Most people think of mammals as the most popular creatures in the animal kingdom. They're often furry and the camera loves them. But some are very strange indeed... and not at all pretty!

The strangest face in the animal kingdom probably belongs to the star-nosed mole, found in North America. The mole's nose has 22 fleshy, highly sensitive tentacles on the end of it – and it looks as strange as it sounds. All moles have poor eyesight but the star-nosed mole's is poor even by mole standards. It uses its strange snout to feel around in the dark and find food – it can identify the food and eat it in less than a quarter of a second.

Australia is home to many weird creatures and the echidna could be the strangest of all. An echidna looks like a large, extra spiky hedgehog, with a long, pointy beak. Most mammals don't lay eggs, but the echidna does. Once the eggs hatch, echidnas carry their babies in pouches, and they can live for more than 50 years. The enchidnas can move each of their spines (prickles) independently or in groups, at will.

The aye aye: its strange looks make some people afraid of it.

Aye ayes are rare nocturnal animals native to the island of Madagascar. They use their long, clawed middle finger to capture the insect larvae they like to eat. Superstitious people have been known to kill them because they're seen as a bad omen. Sadly, the aye aye is now an endangered species, threatened by the destruction of their habitat as well as the people who kill them.

www.austmus.gov.au/mammals

WeiRd PeTs

**Keeping unusual pets is not just a modern phenomenon...
Here are some real-life examples of pets that you wouldn't
want to find curled up on your sofa...**

Tycho Brahe, the
16th-century Danish
astronomer, owned a pet
moose. His friend and
companion the moose met a sad
end. The moose drank too
much beer at a party, fell
down some steps and
died.

Josephine
Beauharnais,
wife of Napoleon
Bonaparte, owned an
orang-utan that
sometimes joined
her at dinner
parties.

Black widows are venomous spiders, but for some reason people still keep them as pets. In 2004, a Berlin man's pet black widow spider, called Bettina, bit and killed him.

If you think cockroaches are cute, you'll be pleased to know there's one species that makes a good pet: the Madagascan hissing cockroach. It grows up to 8 cm (3 in) long (large enough for you to keep tabs on), it can't fly, like other cockroaches can, and it makes an unusual and appealing hissing sound. Thousands of people really do keep these creatures as pets. At least they don't bite!

People who keep reticulated pythons are at risk of being suffocated – these snakes can grow to over 9 m (30 ft) long.

Animal achievements

Sometimes animals display qualities that can make them seem almost human. The animals featured here have all made the headlines with their incredible behaviour.

Fire-fighting dog
Jackson, a Newfoundland dog, survived a housefire in 2007 by sitting in the bath and breathing air from the plughole. Firefighters were amazed to see the dog alive and well – and impressed to find him using an old-fashioned firefighting trick.

Clever Hans

In the early 1900s, Clever Hans was a horse who seemed to be exceptionally intelligent. His trainer would ask him questions like: 'If it's the 10th of the month today, what is next Friday's date?' and Hans would always give the correct answer, using his hoof to tap out a number. But when the case of Clever Hans's incredible intellect was investigated, it was revealed that Hans was simply responding to his trainer's body language. The trainer had no idea he was giving any signals but the horse would tap his hoof until the trainer seemed satisfied. Hans really was pretty smart, just not in the way everyone had thought.

Cool rider

Nong Oui, a frog from Thailand, can do a whole load of cool tricks. He can ride a toy motorbike, and he has developed a reputation for predicting lottery numbers. The frog's owner, Mrs Bamroongtoi, had to move away from her village in 2008 because people won money with the frog's help, then started losing. Mrs Bamroongtoi is convinced that she and Nong Oui communicate.

Extremophiles

There are some places in the world where you'd think nothing could possibly survive – but some creatures do. They're known as "extremophiles".

Snottites

Stalactites are dramatic formations of calcium that drip down from the roofs of caves and look like icicles. In some places, though, what seems to be a stalactite is in fact a snottite. Unlike stalactites, these gooey, dripping structures are actually alive! They hang from the ceilings of sulphur caves, which are foul-smelling, hot and extremely dark. Snottites thrive on the sulphur and very strong acid that's found inside the caves.

Weird worms

Deep down in the depths of the sea lives the Pompeii worm. These creatures are found in hydrothermal vents – cracks in the seabed that spew out superheated water at temperatures of 80°C (176°F). The Pompeii worm, which is 10 cm (4 in) long and has long, red gills on its head that look like tentacles, is the only animal in the world that can survive such high temperatures.

Weird Thing to Do: Grow Your Own Stalactite

You will need: two jam jars, baking soda, a piece of cardboard, string, paperclips and water.

1. Fill two jam jars two-thirds full of warm water.

2. Stir in enough baking soda to make a thick paste. Add some food colouring if you like.

3. On a piece of cardboard, place the jars about 20 cm apart.

4. Attach paperclips to both ends of a piece of string, and put each end in a jar, making sure the string bows in the middle.

Be amazed as a stalactite begins to grow. (This will take a few days.)

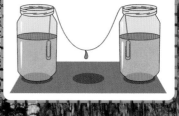

www.astrobiology.com/extreme

Peculiar plants

Foul flowers

The largest single flower in the world is nearly 1 m (3.3 ft) wide and it can weigh up to 11 kg (24 lbs). Its scientific name is *Rafflesia arnoldii* but it's known as the 'corpse flower' because it smells like decaying flesh – flies love it! Another flower, the titan arum is also named 'corpse flower' and it smells even worse.

Meat eaters

Carnivorous plants, like pitcher plants, survive by eating meat. They attract insects by luring them into a sticky, liquid-filled tube from which there is no escape. There are plants that attract bigger victims than just insects, too – some can digest small frogs and birds. There are no plants that are man-eaters, as far as we know...

In southern India, 'tiger trees' are said to grab cows and people with their branches and eat them. The trees are also the prime suspects in cases of tail-less cows in the area. There has not yet been a detailed inquiry.

The Voodoo lily (*Amorphophallus bulbifer*) has a rather unique perfume – it smells like old socks.

The titan arum looks beautiful but smells terrible.

Weird Thing To Do: Bring a Dead Plant Back to Life

You will need: a Rose of Jericho in its dormant state (also known as Dinosaur Plant or Resurrection Plant, scientific name *Anastatica hierochuntica*). It looks like a miniature tumbleweed.

1. Place the plant in a saucer of water.

2. Be amazed as the dried-up weed turns into a luscious green plant.

You can forget to water it again for 50 years and it will still come back to life when you give it water (or get your grandchildren to do it). The plant lives in desert regions and has evolved this way to survive long periods of drought. In fact, the plant has been around for more than 250 million years.

Raining fish and frogs

You're not very likely to be pelted with falling animals during a rainstorm, but it does happen.

Most of the cases reported involve fish, frogs and birds – from ancient Rome to, more recently, a rain of catfish in South Carolina in 1901, a rain of frogs in Croydon, UK in 1998, and a rain of fish in Paracatu, Brazil in 2007. There are various theories for this phenomenon but it's still unexplained. The most likely explanation is that they are caught up and carried by violent winds or waterspouts.

An icy death

In animal rainfalls sometimes the creatures are alive, suggesting that they've been picked up and dropped down again extremely quickly, but sometimes they are dead or encased in ice, which means the animals were probably sucked very high into the air before raining down again.

Rains of fishes

In Honduras, rains of fishes have been reported once or twice a year for over a century. There's even a Festival of the Rain of Fishes every year to celebrate this strange event.

Red rain

There are many fantastical theories to explain red rainfalls – known as 'rains of blood'. Theories range from desert sand storms (sand sometimes has a strong red colour) to rock from volcanoes, or even comets or meteors, mixed with the rain water. Some scientists believe that the rainwater from a red rainfall in southern India in 2001 contained alien life – tiny organisms from outer space that were carried by a comet or meteor. The alien life theory has not yet been proved.

A shower of jellyfish fell on the city of Bath, UK in 1894. In 2007, worms rained on Jennings, Louisiana, USA.

www.fi.edu/weather/

WeiRd LiGhtNiNg

In the 19th century, Tsar Nicholas II of Russia witnessed a 'fiery ball' whizzing around inside a church.

A Swedish magazine used these illustrations in an article on ball lightning in 1925.

Fighter pilots in the Second World War made many reports of glowing lights following their planes. These are thought to be accounts of ball lighting.

In 1994, a tiny ball of lightning broke through a window in Uppsala, Sweden, leaving a 5cm (2 in) circular hole.

Ball lightning is extremely rare, but over the centuries it has been seen in the sky and also inside buildings and aircraft. It is a brightly glowing sphere and no one really knows what causes it.

Factory workers in Gloucestershire, UK, were amazed to see a small ball of light whizzing around their factory: it gave people electric shocks as it passed and hit one woman on - the shoulder.

There are many different theories, both supernatural and scientific, but so far there is no definitive explanation.

Weird Thing To Do: Make Lightning

You will need a piece of woollen cloth, a paperclip and an inflated balloon. This weird thing to do works better if it's a dry day with low humidity.

1. Dim the lights – the darker the better.
2. Rub the balloon against the wool for 30 seconds.
3. Hold it close to the paperclip.
4. Be amazed as lightning sparks between the balloon and the paperclip.

Rubbing the balloon against the wool gives the balloon a negative charge. Holding the balloon near the paperclip makes the paperclip positively charged. The air between the balloon and the paperclip becomes positively charged too – causing a spark.

The mysterious sliding rocks of Death Valley

The world is full of spectacular landscapes, like the Giant's Causeway in Ireland, or Uluru in Australia. But none of them is quite like the marvels of Racetrack Playa, California, USA.

California's Death Valley is one of the hottest places on earth. It's also home to a geological mystery: strange sliding rocks.

The Playa is a remote dry lakebed in Death Valley. It is scattered with rocks of different shapes and sizes – some weighing more than 300 kg (660 lb). The rocks are quite ordinary, apart from one thing: they move.

The case of the sliding rocks gets even stranger: no one has ever actually witnessed the rocks moving. Nevertheless, the evidence is clear to see. The rocks have long trails gouged into the ground behind them. There are no other tracks to suggest that the rocks have been pulled or pushed by people or machinery. The tracks are all slightly different – either straight, curved, or zigzag. The longest is nearly 900 m (3,000 ft) and new tracks appear all the time.

What is the explanation for the sliding rocks? One idea is that the rocks are pulled around by the Earth's magnetism. The latest theory is that the rocks are blown by strong winds after heavy rainfall. The rain makes the Playa surface very slippery. The lack of witnesses mean that this has still not been proved and there is one thing which is a mystery – the tracks seem to show individual rocks moving in different directions. How is this possible if the wind is to blame?

Northern Lights

The Northern Lights are a spectacular natural lightshow at the North Pole, when the sky is illuminated with swirling patterns of green, red and blue. The nearer to the Pole you are, the more likely you are to see them.

Before the cause of the Northern Lights was discovered, people came up with all sorts of interesting explanations. They believed the lights were...

the reflection of a huge shoal of herrings...

the souls of dead warriors...

angry gods...

swishing tails of foxes made of fire.

In fact, the lights appear in the sky becaue of 'solar wind' – when flares and explosions from the Sun throw charged particles into space. Solar wind reacts with the Earth's upper atmosphere at each end of its magnetic field (the North and South Poles) releasing energy as light.

Weird Thing To Do: Make a Rainbow in a Dark Room

You will need: a clear plastic box, a torch, a mirror, sticky tape, white card and black card.

1. Make a mask out of black card for the front of your torch with a small slit in the centre – stick it to the torch with sticky tape.

2. Half fill the box with water.

3. Lean the mirror inside the box against one end.

4. Shine the torch at the mirror through the water-filled box.

5. Hold up the white card to catch the reflection from the mirror.

6. Be astounded at the rainbow on the white card.

This works because the seven different colours that make up light all travel at different speeds, and so each one bends at a different angle when light is refracted through the water. The mirror reflects the different colours onto the card separately – making a rainbow!

METEORITES AND STAR JELLY

Every so often a huge lump of rock hurtles through space and comes crashing down towards Earth. Only the biggest and hardest ones make it through the Earth's atmosphere without being burnt up – these are known as meteorites.

Most meteorites start off spinning around in the Asteroid Belt between Jupiter and Mars. At this stage, many meotorites are huge but most are small by the time they reach Earth (thankfully). When a big one does get through, the force makes a crater on the surface of the earth. So far, about 120 meteorite craters have been discovered.

No one is known to have been killed by a meteorite. One woman came close when a meteorite crashed through the roof of her house while she was sitting on the sofa. The meteorite bashed her on the leg, causing a nasty bruise.

A huge meteorite is one theory for the extinction of dinosaurs – an enormous crater in Central America dates from about the right time.

'Star jelly' is a strange phenomenon associated with meteorite falls and meteor showers (shooting stars). Unexplained, foul-smelling, gelatinous blobs have been found on the ground, often directly after seeing a shooting star or a meteorite fall. In 1696, the philosopher Henry More decided it was the 'excrement' of shooting stars. Recent examples include blobs of purple gloop in Texas following a meteor shower in 1979, translucent goo scattered in puddles around Hobart, Australia, following a shooting star in 1996, and a strange jelly object that fell in U-Thai Thani, Thailand in 2006.

'Star jelly' has not yet been successfully analysed and it might not have anything to do with the meteorites at all. One theory is that it is semi-digested frog spawn that's been vomited up by an animal.

Biodynamics

Biodynamics is a way of farming – like organic farming, no pesticides or manufactured chemicals are used. But biodynamic farmers go a bit further than that – and they enlist the help of the moon...

Biodynamic farming involves some rather strange preparations for the soil. You might want to try this in your garden: fill a cow's horn with cow manure and bury it in the ground in autumn. Dig it up the next spring, stir a teaspoon of it into 50 l (13 gallons) of water and scatter it across the ground every other minute.

Other biodynamic preparations include chamomile flowers inside a length of cow intestine, bark in animal skulls, and yarrow flowers inside the bladder of a male deer.

Biodynamic farming includes rules about when different crops should be planted. Different phases of the moon benefit different farming activities, such as sowing, planting or harvesting. There are also astrological rules: for example, carrots and other root vegetables should only be planted during an earth sign of the zodiac.

Studies show that biodynamic farming produces similar results to organic farming. But there *is* evidence to suggest that the cycles of the moon do affect plant growth: the moon affects tides and the moisture in soil, and there seems to be evidence of seeds germinating faster if they're planted when the moon is full.

WeiRd FoSsiLs

In 2003, on the island of Flores in Indonesia, scientists uncovered one of the most exciting fossil finds of recent years: Homo floresiensis. The fossils are the skull and other remains of a human-like creature. The creature seems to have been not much more than 1 m (3 ft) tall, and lived at the same time as modern humans. The little people have been nicknamed 'hobbits' but whether this really is a new species of human or not is the subject of heated debate.

In 2007, scientists discovered the fossilised remains of the largest creepy-crawly ever. The creature, *Jaekelopterus rhenaniae*, is a sea scorpion with eight legs and two enormous claws. It measured more than 2.4 m (8 ft) and weighed over 180 kg (400 lb).

Weird Thing To Do: Make Your Own Fake Fossil

You need: an object to fossilise – a leaf, a shell, small plastic toy, some made-up plaster of Paris (nice and thick), petroleum jelly, a piece of cardboard.

1. Form the plaster of Paris into a square or rectangle shape 2-3 cm (1 in) deep on the cardboard.

2. Coat your object in petroleum jelly and press into the mixture until it's half-submerged.

3. Leave it to dry in a warm place.

4. Remove the object and marvel at your fossil.

This is one of the ways that real fossils form – when plants or animal remains became coated in mud. Over millions of years, the mud turns to stone but the leaf or animal rots away, leaving a 'cast'.

This strange looking fossil is a lambeosaurus, discovered in 1914. The dinosaur's head crest helped its sense of smell and made sounds to warn off predators.

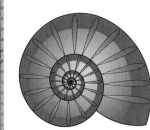

Ghostly tales

Do you believe that the spirits of the dead can return to Earth to haunt the living? Many people do, and there are thousands of tales of ghostly apparitions.

One of the most famous American ghost stories is about the Bell Witch, a ghost said to have terrorised the Bell family for several years in 19th century Tennessee. When Mr Bell died, a ghostly voice claimed that it was responsible... before singing a cheerful song about a bottle of brandy.

Sometimes the most unlikely places seem to be haunted. In Sunnyvale, California, USA, the local toyshop is reported to be haunted by the ghost of Johnny Johnson, who died in 1884 on the spot where the store now stands. Johnny died from a nasty accident with an axe. In 2007, a librarian called for an exorcist to rid Gravesend library in Kent, UK, of a ghost who flushes the toilet 'when he thinks everybody's gone home'.

Roman soldiers, ghostly ladies and a phantom lorry have all been reported on the M6 motorway, which is apparently Britain's most haunted road.

Hear the fear

Perhaps ghost sightings can be explained by weird sounds. An engineer called Vic Tandy became terrified while working in his lab one evening, and even thought he saw something grey and ghostly. He discovered that a fan in his laboratory was producing infrasound – sound frequencies below the range of human hearing. Could this have been making him feel so frightened? He found that particular infrasound frequencies can make people and animals feel uneasy, anxious, dizzy and even cause panic attacks. More recent research suggests that electromagnetic forces, which can be caused by infrasound, might be the root cause of the feeling of fear.

Talking to ghosts

'Spirit mediums' claim to have the ability to communicate with ghosts. Some say they hear the dead speaking and relate what they say, some write down messages, and others seem to fall into a trance and speak as if the dead person were speaking through them.

Communicating with the dead was especially popular in the 19th century. The Fox sisters, from New York State in America, were among the first to make a living from it. The ghosts usually communicated through rapping noises. After many years, one Fox sister gave a public demonstration of how she really produced the sounds – by cracking the bones in her toes.

Spirit mediums claimed that they used a mysterious substance called ectoplasm, which gave the ghost a physical form. Helen Duncan, a British medium, was investigated by a researcher who discovered that she produced ectoplasm by swallowing a strange mixture and then regurgitating it. It was made of cheesecloth, safety pins, rubber gloves and (probably) egg white.

Weird Thing To Do: Make Your Own Ectoplasm

You need: borax powder (find it in the supermarket near the washing powder), PVA glue, food colouring and water.

1. Measure 275 ml (9 fluid oz.) water in a jug and add 3 tablespoons of borax.

2. In a separate bowl, mix 5 spoons of glue with the same amount of water and a few drops of food colouring (the colour you think your ghost would like).

3. Add the borax solution a teaspoon at a time, stirring thoroughly each time.

4. Eventually it will be thick enough to pick up. If it's too sticky, rinse off the excess glue with water.

5. Form your ghost.

Note: DON'T eat your ectoplasm!

HaUNtED hOusE

All ghosts need somewhere to rattle their chains, walk through walls and moan horribly. Most haunt the place where they met their terrible fate. If you like to be scared stiff, pay a visit to Glamis Castle in Scotland. It's supposed to be one of the most haunted buildings in the world...

The castle is the setting for Shakespeare's play *Macbeth*. King Malcolm II of Scotland, who is murdered in the play, really *was* murdered here in 1018 and is said to haunt the building.

There are reports of a ghostly butler in a room known as 'Hangman's Chamber'.

The ghost of a woman with a bleeding mouth is said to haunt the grounds. Some say she is a vampire, while others tell the tale of a servant whose tongue was cut out to stop her speaking of a crime she witnessed.

The story goes that a towel was once hung from every window in the castle. From the outside a window without a towel was visible but the room could not be found. The secret room is supposed to contain a dreadful secret or even a monster.

The 'Mad Earl's Walk' on the castle ramparts is said to have been the place where a locked up boy was allowed to exercise... and some say he still does.

A ghost known as Jack the Runner is said to haunt the grounds on moonlit nights.

In one of the castle rooms, the furniture is reported to transform into antiques from a past age.

There are many reports of a Grey Lady in the chapel and above the clock tower. She is thought to be the ghost of Lady Janet Douglas, burned as a witch in 1537.

The phantom of cruel Earl Beardie is said to play cards in a secret room for eternity. Others say his ghost wanders the castle at night.

www.glamis-castle.co.uk

BIG CATS

If you hear a spine-chilling roar when you are out on the remote moors of southwest England you could be in danger of meeting the Beast of Bodmin Moor.

There have been hundreds of reports of a big cat, like a leopard or a puma, on the loose in Cornwall. The animal has been blamed for killing sheep, chickens and other farm livestock.

Over the last 20 years, three big cat skulls have been discovered near Bodmin Moor. Two were found to be big cat skulls that had been taken from leopard skin rugs, and the other had been taken from a stuffed big cat. In 1995, a government report into sightings of the creature found no evidence for its existence, but claimed sightings continue. There's also a Beast of Exmoor – one Devon farmer claimed to have lost over a hundred sheep to the creature.

Sightings of the 'Catgarookey' were recently reported in Britain. In 2005, the strange animal – described as a cross between a big cat, a kangaroo and a monkey – was said to be roaming the streets of Salisbury in Wiltshire.

No real evidence for any of these creatures has ever been found. Some people believe this is because the creatures are supernatural 'ghost cats' – a feline equivalent of the terrifying 'Black Dogs' of folklore.

Black Dogs inhabit Europe and North and South America. They don't usually harm people directly, but the belief is that if you see the glowing, red eyes of a black dog it means you are about to die.

Mythical beasts

Chupacabras

If you ever spot a greyish-green creature, about 1 m (3.3 ft) tall, with sharp fangs, a dog-like face, leathery skin and a row of spines down its back, you're probably looking at the Chupacabras (Spanish for 'goat-sucker'). There have been reports of this creature since 1995 in South America, Mexico and the United States – and, more recently, in Russia. The hallmark of the Chupacabras is to leave dead animals, completely drained of blood, in its wake.

Inashi

If the Chupacabras sounds scary, you definitely wouldn't want to meet the Inashi. It's a 5 m- (16.5 ft-) tall, one-eyed, hairy, apelike creature which is said to wander the Brazilian rainforest, followed by swarms of flies due to its foul odour. The Inashi twists off people's skulls and sucks out their brains. It sounds rather like the other, more famous, apelike creatures – Bigfoot in North America and the Yeti in the Himalayas – apart from the brain-sucking bit.

Mokele Mbembe

The Mokele Mbembe (which can be translated as 'he who stops rivers') is supposed to roam the Congo River Basin in Central Africa. It's said to be the size of an elephant and resembles a dinosaur. Some people believe this could be an actual dinosaur that somehow survived. The creature is a vegetarian, you'll be pleased to know, although it has supposedly killed people and hippos. Sightings of Mokele Mbembe continue to the present day.

UFOs

There have been hundreds of thousands of reports of Unidentified Flying Objects. Some, of course, turn out to be identified flying objects, but many remain unexplained.

Descriptions of UFOs vary widely: some are triangular, some are cigar-shaped, disc-shaped, spherical, dome-shaped, egg-shaped, and others are moving balls of light. Some move erratically, some hover, others whizz along at incredible speeds. The two most popular explanations are alien spacecraft and secret aircraft or weapon experimentation by humans. Or maybe they are giant invisible creatures that live in Earth's upper atmosphere... This last theory was developed by Trevor Constable – he thought the creatures were probably ancient inhabitants of Earth, that were around even before the planet became solid, and 'of low intelligence'.

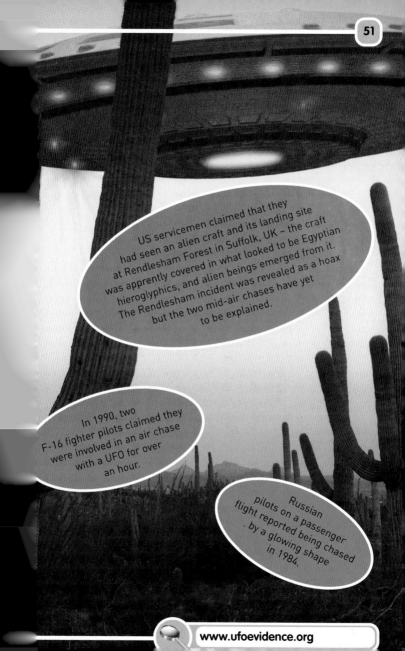

US servicemen claimed that they had seen an alien craft and its landing site at Rendlesham Forest in Suffolk, UK – the craft was apprently covered in what looked to be Egyptian hieroglyphics, and alien beings emerged from it. The Rendlesham incident was revealed as a hoax but the two mid-air chases have yet to be explained.

In 1990, two F-16 fighter pilots claimed they were involved in an air chase with a UFO for over an hour.

Russian pilots on a passenger flight reported being chased . by a glowing shape in 1984.

Alien encounters

Some people claim not only to have seen UFOs, but to have made contact with their extra-terrestrial passengers...

In 1976, four men were on a canoeing trip in Maine, USA. While out fishing at night, the men said they spotted a big glowing sphere hovering over the trees, which fired a beam of light at them. The next they knew they were near the bank watching the object disappear and several hours had passed. Under hypnosis, the men all remembered being taken into an alien craft, where bald, blank-eyed aliens carried out medical examinations on them all.

In 2005, locals in the town of Aracruz, Brazil saw a fireball in the sky. More than 50 people called the police, many believing they were witnessing an invasion. A badly burnt alien body was found and taken to hospital. Doctors were unable to treat the patient, which turned out to be a burnt rubber doll. The town had been the victim of a hoax.

A lawyer in Dresden advertised himself as 'Germany's first alien abduction laywer' in 2006. He tries to get compensation from the state for people who believe they have been abducted by UFOs, and also investigates whether these people are really the victims of human abuse. So far he has had few clients for his new line of business.

Some alien abductions have witnesses: in 2001, a woman in Gundiah, Australia, claimed she watched as her friend was transported through an open window on a beam of light coming from a UFO. Just 90 minutes later the abductee was found nearly 800 km (500 mi) away – she appeared to have eaten nothing for days and remembered a masked man and a darkened room.

THE LIVING DEAD

In folklore, a zombie is a dead person who has been reanimated by supernatural power. You might have seen one at the movies, but hopefully nowhere else! They're famous for shuffling about slowly with outstretched arms and a dead-eyed stare, sporting torn clothing and horrible wounds. Do these horror-film monsters have some basis in reality?

In 1988, a 17-year-old Haitian boy called Wilfred Doricent became very ill and died. A doctor signed his death certificate and he was buried in an above-ground concrete tomb. Wilfred later turned up at a village event – alive, but not able to speak or remember much about his past. Many people believed that Wilfred's father had made an enemy of a powerful Voodoo priest, who had made Wilfred into a zombie and taken his soul.

Perhaps someone poisoned Wilfred with tetrodotoxin, a poison found in pufferfish, which can make victims appear dead even though they are conscious of everything going on around them. One ex-Voodoo practitioner has claimed that this is how Voodoo priests convince people of their supernatural powers. Wilfred could have been deprived of oxygen while in his tomb, causing the damage to his brain that destroyed his memory and his speech. But this doesn't explain how he managed to escape from his concrete tomb...

Vampires are dead
bodies that rise from
their coffins at night and suck
blood from living human beings
with their sharp fangs. At least,
that's one version: Chinese
vampires have red eyes and green
or pink hair, Greek ones are
half-woman, half-winged snake,
and the Malaysian blood-sucking
Penanggalang is a flying head.

www.monstrous.com

Spontaneous Human Combustion

Spontaneous Human Combustion (SHC) is the name given to cases of human beings bursting into flames for no obvious reason. Often the human body itself is burnt to a cinder, while the area around them remains untouched by fire.

One famous case of SHC happened in 1951, when Mary Reeser's body was found in her living room: only her foot was untouched – the rest of her body was completely burnt. The room was hardly damaged by the fire. A possible explanation is known as the 'wick effect', which compares the human body to a candle. The human body contains enough flammable material to burn like a candle – if the right conditions are present, and if something sets the body alight. Perhaps this is what happened to Mary Reeser - it was discovered that the victim had taken sleeping pills and had been smoking.

Another suspected case of SHC had a witness: in 1982, Jeannie Saffin caught fire while sitting in the kitchen with her father at his London home. She was rushed to hospital but died soon afterwards, having suffered terrible burns to her face and hands. Sceptics point out that Jeannie had been smoking (though she wasn't when her father saw the flames) and a spark from the cigarette could have been smouldering in her clothing.

Cigarettes can't be used to explain away every case of SHC. In 1998, 82-year-old Agnes Phillips began to burn while sitting in a parked car in New South Wales, Australia. Her daughter saw smoke and dragged her from the car, but she died in hospital a week later. Neither woman smoked and there was nothing wrong with the car.

Levitation

Levitation is the strange phenomenon of people or objects rising into the air and floating about without any physical support. Maybe you've gasped in amazement as a stage magician mysteriously hovered above the ground, for example. But you might not be too surprised to learn that magicians don't really rise into the air by magic: it's just a clever illusion.

In 1936, Indian Yogi Pullavar appeared to hover for four minutes in front of a crowd of 150 people.

Flying monks

There are plenty of claims of levitation by means of a supernatural force. Joseph of Copertino was a 17th century Italian monk who would fall into a religious trance and soar into the air, to the amazement of onlookers. Many Christian saints are believed to be capable of levitation. Hindu priests and Japanese ninjas (skilled assassins) have also been reported to hover or fly. And there are claims of 'yogic flying', in which people use meditation to make themselves physically rise into the air.

Feel the force

It really is possible to make objects hover in midair without the involvement of any supernatural forces: all you need is a force pushing upwards equal to the weight of the object. Magnetic levitation, for example, uses the force of a magnetic field to make things float above ground – this is how maglev trains work. Electrical charges and jets of air can also be used to make things levitate.

Russian Poster for Mysterious Hindu Linga Sing

Weird Thing to Do: Make Your Arms Levitate

1. Stand in a doorway.

2. Press the back of each hand against the door frame and push.

3. Push really hard – put some effort into it! - and continue to do so for at least 30 seconds.

4. Walk away from the doorframe and relax your muscles. Be astonished as your arms float upwards effortlessly!

This works because pushing hard releases calcium into your muscles to make them move – but they can't because the door frame's in the way. By the time you step away from the door frame and relax the muscles in your arms, a lot of calcium has been released and not used - so your arms move, even though your brain has stopped sending the message.

www.levitation.org

CROP CIRCLES

The weird crop patterns puzzled everybody when they began appearing in fields in England in the 1970s. How did they get there? Who made them? And why?

Crop circles are spectacular geometrical patterns made by flattening wheat, barley or other crops in farmers' fields. Some are extremely complicated, some are enormous, all look very strange indeed.

Then, in 1991, the strange secret was revealed: two blokes called Doug and Dave had been creating them using planks, wire and rope. They'd sneak into fields at night, go about their work, and leave everyone flummoxed at daybreak. Just for a laugh! Since then other crop circle makers have come forward and some have demonstrated their work.

Some crop circle enthusiasts don't believe that all crop circles are made by people like Doug and Dave.

In fact, they don't believe they're made by people at all: they are the weird work of beings from far-off planets. Either the circles are the aliens' attempts at communication, or the results of spacecraft take-off and landing.

Others claim that the circles are the result of some kind of supernatural activity, since crop circles tend to appear near to stone circles or ancient burial sites. Another theory suggests that the patterns are made by freak winds and other strange weather phenomena.

Ever more beautiful and intricate crop circles appear all over the world, including 3D designs. Human creators continue to come forward: so far there have been no claims from outer space or beyond the grave.

www.circlemakers.org

TIME TRAVEL

Have you ever wondered if it might be possible to travel in time? Think about all the things you could do – like finding the winning lottery number! Einstein's Theory of Relativity showed that, in theory, it is possible. But scientists still argue about whether or not we will ever travel through time.

One problem with travelling back in time is that you could end up altering events so that you are never born. Then what would happen? Would you instantly disappear? Some people think this paradox makes time travel impossible.

Some people believe they have already managed to travel through time – without even trying! Two English married couples on holiday together in France claimed that they stayed for a night in a strange, old-fashioned hotel that they could never find again. They were further mystified when they realised that all of the photographs they took at the hotel had disappeared from the roll of film. The incident was explained as a time slip.

An American man, Steven Gibbs, calls himself a 'time traveller' and claims that he has already invented a time machine. The machine, which he has named the "Hyper Dimensional Resonator", allows the user to 'spontaneously astral project'. In fact, you can buy one for just US $590. Gibbs says he was given plans for his machine by time-travelling aliens.

Since the 1990s, various people have reported strange slips of time in central Liverpool. They are mysteriously transported to the 1950s or 1960s for a few minutes, before being returned to the present day, just as mysteriously.

Unsolved mysteries

Mysterious things happen all over the world. Rational explanations are found for many of them, but some continue to defy explanation...

Ghost ship

The story of the Marie Celeste is one of the world's most famous unsolved mysteries. The ship, carrying the captain, his wife and daughter and seven crew members, picked up a cargo of industrial alcohol in New York and set off for Italy in November 1872. A month later, another ship spotted the Marie Celeste drifting in the Straits of Gibraltar and sent out a boarding party. The ship was in good condition, still carrying its cargo... but with no sign of the ten people who should have been on board. They were never found.

In 2006, scientists at University College London built a replica of the Marie Celeste's hold and simulated an explosion caused by leaking alcohol. Because alcohol burns at a low temperature, the experiment produced a wave of flame with cool air behind it, so that there was no burning or even scorching. We'll probably never know what happened, but it could be that an explosion caused the captain and crew to abandon ship.

Weird hum

The 'Taos Hum' is a low-pitched noise, like the sound of a distant engine. The strange thing is that no one knows what is making the noise. It's been reported in different locations all over the world – including Taos in New Mexico, USA, from where it gets its name. Not everyone can hear the Hum, but those who do say it's maddening. The residents of Taos were so upset by it that they demanded a government investigation, but the scientists who investigated in 1997 didn't find an answer. The sound could be caused by electromagnetic transmitters (an element of wireless technology). The mystery remains unsolved.

Weird lights

The Marfa Lights are seen several times a year, about 15 km (9 mi) east of the town of Marfa, Texas, USA. Reports say that the lights, usually white, yellow, orange or red, bounce around the sky, vanish and reappear. They have yet to be explained, but various theories include ghosts, swamp gas, ball lightning, and a mirage caused by rising hot air. Some people say that its simply the lights from cars on the nearby highway.

The Voynich Manuscript

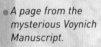

A page from the mysterious Voynich Manuscript.

Code or cipher?

A code substitutes complete words but a cipher substitutes each individual letter with a symbol or another letter. The Voynich Manuscript is probably a cipher rather than a code.

In 1912, Wilfrid Voynich bought an old illustrated book, written in an unknown language and an unknown alphabet. Since no one can read it, its illustrations are the only clues to what the book is about: it includes one section on plants (unlike any plants that are around today), one on stars and planets, another that is full of drawings of pipes and tubes (this could be about the human body), and another that might be a calendar.

The mixture of familiar and strange letttters and numbers that the book is written in is believed to be a sort of code, though no one has ever been able to crack it. The Voynich Manuscript's weird illustrations and strange text remain a mystery.

Weird Thing To Do: Send a Secret Cipher

Here's a cipher you can use to send secret messages. It looks cool too! Can you decipher this one?

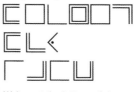

1. Write out the letters of the alphabet in boxes, like this:

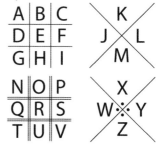

2. You'll see that each letter is enclosed by a different 'pen'. (The cipher is sometimes known as 'pig pen'.) The letter S is enclosed by a pen this shape:

3. Use your cipher to send top secret information.

Answer: Secret Spy Info

www.voynich.nu

Coincidence

Some coincidences are so amazing that people wonder if they really are just coincidences. Could it be that some strange force is at work?

In 1992, the strange case of a young man's death was reported. He jumped from the top of his 26-storey apartment building and was shot on the way down by a bullet fired from a gun aimed at a woman inside the building. The man who fired the gun claimed that he was aiming the gun at his wife but had no idea the gun was loaded – he and his wife kept an unloaded gun and sometimes pointed it at one another and pulled the trigger as a joke. The man was telling the truth. Some weeks earlier, their son had loaded the gun in an attempt to kill one of them. But the son had eventually decided to commit suicide – and jumped from the top of the apartment building.

In 2002, twin 71-year-old brothers were both killed on the same road in very similar bicycle accidents just hours apart. The police officer investigating the deaths said: 'It made my hair stand on end'. A similar coincidence happened in 1976 when a man was killed by a taxi while riding a moped, just as his brother had been a year before – it was the same moped, the same taxi, the same driver and even the same passenger in the taxi.

The Earth is inhabited by billions of people, over millions of kilometres. Some coincidences seem incredible but every second holds infinite possibilities for what might happen. These things are often called coincidences, but wouldn't it be even weirder if they didn't happen?

LUCK

Do you consider yourself lucky or unlucky? Or do you think there's no such thing as luck? There are some amazing tales of fortunate and unfortunate people...

Unlucky seven

Roy Sullivan was a forest ranger at Shenandoah National Park in Virginia, USA, for most of his life. He was struck by lightning seven times – in 1942, 1969, 1970, 1972, 1973, 1974 and 1977. He survived all seven strikes, though he did lose his toenails, eyebrows and hair. The chances of being struck that many times are billions and billions to one.

Headache cure

In 2005, a retired school teacher turned up in a Polish hospital complaining of a headache. He had fallen over in his kitchen a few days earlier. Doctors discovered a 12 cm (5 in) knife blade embedded in the man's head. Amazingly, it had missed all vital nerves, blood vessels and bones. The man said he'd wondered what had happened to his knife when he could only find the handle. Surgeons removed the blade in a short operation, and the incident caused the man no lasting damage.

Lucky or unlucky?

In the 1960s a Croatian man called Frane Selak jumped into an icy river to save himself after his train crashed and killed 17 passengers. A year later, the door blew off the plane he was travelling in and he was sucked out. The plane then crashed, killing 19 people. Selak was found in a haystack with only minor injuries. A few years later he was involved in a bus accident that killed four people. In 1970 his car caught fire – he got out seconds before it exploded. Then, in 1973 a faulty fuel pump in a different car sprayed flaming petrol through the air vents as Selak was driving – again, he survived with only minor injuries. Nothing terrible happened to Selak for 20 years or so, then in 1995 he was hit by a bus and the following year he was forced to leap from his car – he landed in a tree and watched his car plummet 100 metres down a mountainside where it burst into flames. In 2003, aged 74, Selak bought his first lottery ticket in 40 years and won over US $1 million. In 2004 he was asked to fly to Australia to film a TV commercial: he declined because he didn't want to push his luck.

www.ancient-symbols.com/good_luck_symbols.html

CURSES

The Scottish Play

Many actors are convinced that there's a curse on performances of Shakespeare's play *Macbeth*, and refuse to speak its name inside a theatre for fear the curse will strike. The story goes that Shakespeare used real witches' spells for his three witch characters. In one production in 1942, three actors, the costume designer and the set designer all died. A riot in a theatre caused 31 deaths during another performance. In 1970, an American performance saw the young actor playing the lead suddenly die of a heart attack on stage. Nevertheless, the play is often performed without any tragic events.

The Presidents' Curse

There is said to be a curse targeting US presidents that follows a 20-year pattern:

1840 President Harrison elected. Harrison died of pneumonia in 1841.

1860 Abraham Lincoln elected. He was assassinated in 1865.

1880 President Garfield elected. Garfield was shot and killed in 1881.

1900 William McKinley re-elected president. He was assassinated in 1901.

1920 Warren G Harding elected. Harding died of a heart attack in 1923.

1940 Franklin D Roosevelt began his third term as president. He died just after starting his fourth term in 1945,

1960 John F. Kennedy became president. In 1963, Kennedy was assassinated.

1980 Ronald Reagan elected. He cheated death when an assassin's bullet just missed his heart.

The story goes that Tecumseh, a Native American Indian chief who was defeated in battle by William Henry Harrison, put a curse on the 'Great White Fathers'. Another version of the story says it was a different Indian – Tenskawatawa. If there ever was a curse, Ronald Reagan's survival must have broken it – the president elected in 2000 was George W Bush.

DANGEROUS SCIENCE

It seems that some scientists will stop at nothing in the interests of science and discovery. They risk becoming blind and deaf and some even risk their lives.

Isaac Newton, one of the most famous scientists of all time, nearly blinded himself by poking sticks into his eye sockets. He was performing experiments about colour.

Stubbins Ffirth, a doctor in Philadelphia, USA in the 1800s, was convinced that the deadly disease yellow fever was not contagious. He believed it was caused by too much heat, food and noise. To prove it, he cut his arm and poured vomit from a yellow-fever patient into the wound. He didn't get the disease, so he went further: he poured vomit into his eyes and he actually ate a yellow-fever patient's vomit. He *still* didn't get the disease. After all that, Ffirth was actually wrong: yellow fever is contagious, but it needs to be passed into the blood stream, usually by the bite of a mosquito.

French scientist Pierre Dulong discovered the explosive nitrogen trichloride in 1811. During his experiments he dissolved his eyeball and two of his fingers.

Dr Robert A Lopez published the results of his investigations into cats' ear mites in 1993. He experimented by transplanting mites from cats' ears into his own ears and these were his results: 'I heard scratching sounds, then moving sounds, as the mites began to explore my ear canal. Itching sensations then started, and all three sensations merged into a weird cacophony of sound and pain'. It seems that his main discovery was that having mites in your ears is very unpleasant indeed.

REVOLTING SCIENCE

Some scientists are so interested in their work that nothing puts them off – no matter how sick-makingly horrible the experiment might be.

Hennig Brand discovered the chemical element phosphorus in 1669, after a long and unpleasant series of experiments that involved 50 buckets of human urine for each one.

During the 1700s, Lazzaro Spallanzani investigated how food changed inside the body. His experiment involved eating, vomiting and then eating the vomit. He even went so far as to eat vomit he'd already vomited up twice before.

Modern scientists continue to devise gruesome experiments. In 1992, researchers at the Japanese Shiseido Research Centre made a long and revolting study of the chemical compounds responsible for foot odour. Scientists took samples from smelly socks and feet and tested them for fatty acids.

Canadian scientist Dr Wassersug was interested in Costa Rican tadpoles, and their chances of survival depending on how they taste. There was only one way for Dr Wassersug to find out: a tadpole taste-test, carried out in 2000.

Weird Thing To Do: Grow a Bacteria Colony

To conduct your own revolting experiment, you will need: Petri dishes, nutrient agar (ask your science teacher) and cotton buds.

1) Make up the nutrient agar according to the instructions. You need just a thin layer of it in your Petri dishes.

2) Bacteria is found all over the place – human skin, a pet's hair, the surface of the sink. Choose some different sources for your bacteria and put one kind into each of the Petri dishes (e.g. hair in one, bacteria on the cotton bud in another).

3) Label the lids and put them on the dishes.

4) Leave them for a day or two in a warm place.

5) Observe your bacteria colonies with horror.

Bacteria can be dangerous in large quantities. Don't remove the lids from the dishes. When you've been horrified enough, ask an adult to carefully remove the lids wearing rubber gloves and pour bleach on the agar before throwing them away.

sink

sink

Creature treatments

Ant bites

In ancient India, ants were used to stitch wounds together. The head of the ant would be held next to the wound to let the ant take a bite, then the body would be nipped off, leaving the head attached to the skin to keep the wound closed. Doctors don't use these strange stitches any more – so don't be tempted if you ever spot a giant ant.

Writhing maggots

If you saw a wound crawling with maggots you would probably react with horror. But it turns out that maggots are extremely effective at cleaning nasty wounds. As well as getting rid of rotten flesh and reducing pus, the wriggling creatures seem to help the healing process. Scientists are interested in exactly how the maggots help but this method of treatment is rare – patients seem to prefer antibiotics! As bacteria becomes more and more resistant to antibiotics, let's hope maggots make a comeback.

Blood suckers

Back in the Middle Ages, doctors put blood-sucking leeches onto patients' skin, believing that a good 'bleed' was the answer to many different medical conditions. Leeches are still used today, though not in quite the same way: leeches produce hirudin, which stops blood from clotting, so the creatures are used in surgery. They are especially useful for keeping blood flowing when body parts are reattached.

www.leeches.biz/medicine-leech.htm

Weird inventions

Can you think of something you'd like to be invented – like healthy chocolate, for example? How about a machine to see through solid objects or a phone that fits inside your tooth?

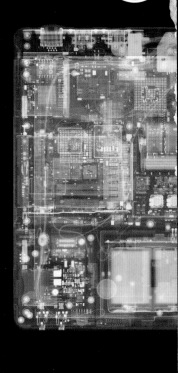

X-ray specs

Canadian Troy Hurtubise claims to have invented a ray that can see through solid objects. His invention fires a ray called 'Angel Light' that makes solid objects transparent – even concrete and lead. The ray has some worrying side effects though: it destroys electronics and can seriously damage any living thing in its path - it's been responsible for the deaths of the inventor's goldfish, and Hurtubise himself became very ill. The Angel Light hasn't yet been demonstrated in public, and many people suspect that the invention is an elaborate hoax. Hurtubise's other inventions include a material known as 'Fire Paste' that is capable of withstanding extremely high temperatures yet cools very quickly, and a grizzly-bear-proof suit.

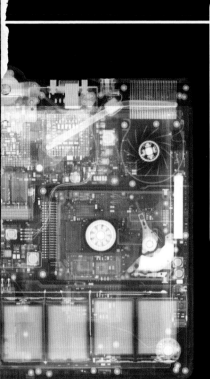

Talking teeth

Two British researchers, James Auger and Jimmy Loizeau, developed a tiny phone that can be embedded inside a tooth. The signals are turned into vibrations that travel to the inner ear – only the person with the tooth phone can hear them. This technology, developed in 2002, has yet to become mainstream but the possibilities seem huge – very soon, you might be able to take calls, listen to music, or be woken up by an alarm clock, all inside your own head.

An invention patented in 2006 claims to cure hiccups by giving the sufferer a mild electric shock.

Crazy inventions

There have been plenty of inventions that haven't caught on. The Smoker's Hat, for example, sucks up cigarette smoke, filters and deodorises it and even adds perfume. Unfortunately, it's not an attractive accessory and it doesn't make smoking any healthier.

TRANSPORT

People have come up with some very unusual ways of getting about, from planes that look like alien spacecraft to coffins on wheels.

Flying saucers

Many UFO sightings describe strange, disc-shaped objects – these could be weird aircraft inventions created by humans over the years. One of the first was the Vought Disc-form Aircraft, which was made in 1911 but never flew. In the 1950s, the Avro-car was designed to take off vertically and reach an incredible speed of 2,400 km/h (1500 mph). After spending £10 million and carrying out years of research, an impressive-looking disc-shaped aircraft was produced but it never got more than about 1.5 m (5 ft) off the ground. English designer Frank Sharman has been more successful with his cigar-shaped and disc-shaped airships – they have flown successfully and were the cause of a number of UFO reports in the 1990s. Even Sharman's airships have never been comercially produced, so no disc-shaped aircraft has ever really taken off. At least, not on planet Earth.

There is a town in Colorado, USA, where they hold an annual coffin race. The race is in memory of a woman who was buried on the summit of Red Mountain. Years later, the soil eroded and her coffin was washed down the mountain and all the way into town. Modern competitors zoom along the town's main street in wheeled coffins.

Wacky races

The Lawnmower Racing Championship began as an April Fool's joke in 1992, but was so popular that it's held every year in Lake Mendota, USA. An even weirder sight is the annual pedal-powered car race in Valentigney, France. Drivers *and* cars must wear imaginative costumes: monkey drivers in banana cars and witches driving pumpkins are recent examples.

Record-breaking sofa

A motorized sofa holds the record for the fastest furniture in the world, with a top speed of 140 km/h (90 mph) – and it's licensed to be driven on UK roads, so watch out for it.

www.manitousprings.org/coffin_races.htm

Future fashion

If you're looking for a fashion statement that will really make you stand out from the crowd, read on...

Researchers at Georgia Tech in the US have developed a smart shirt, made of special fibres that enable the shirt to communicate wirelessly with other computers. In Europe, a musical jacket has been developed by the MIT Media Lab: it has a fabric keypad connected to a synthesizer. Scientists are also trying to manufacture a fabric that can generate its own power as it moves.

Invisible clothes

Professor Susumu Tachi has developed a coat that appears to make the wearer invisible. It's made with a special 'retro-reflective' material that acts as a screen – images from a camera behind the coat are projected on to it, making it look as if the coat and the wearer are completely transparent. Professor Tachi didn't invent this for fashion – it could be used by surgeons to see behind their hands and instruments during surgery, or by pilots to see the ground beneath their cockpits. Now even windowless rooms could have a view.

Odour-eating clothes

A US company has developed underpants that can disguise horrible smells. The pants have a multilayered filter that prevents pongs from escaping. A French company has gone even further: they have invented a material that can disguise body odour for up to a month.

Professor Tachi in the invisibility coat.

One day, clothing may be able to do many of the same jobs as phones and computers.

Optical illusions

What you see isn't always what you get. Your brain can be tricked quite easily into thinking you're seeing something you're not.

Necker cube

This cube looks simple but it's actually not: it doesn't show which lines are in front and which are behind. Your brain will interpret it one way or the other – either seen from above or below. If you try, you can see it both ways.

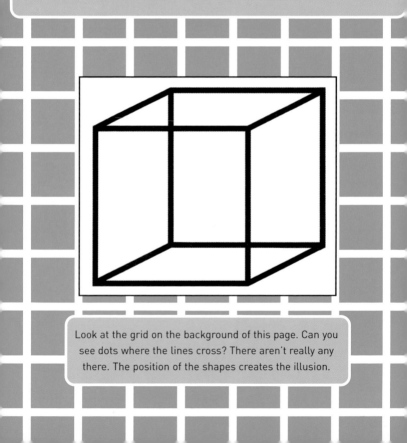

Look at the grid on the background of this page. Can you see dots where the lines cross? There aren't really any there. The position of the shapes creates the illusion.

Cafe wall

The lines on this image appear to be slanting, but in fact they are all parallel. It's an illusion caused by the grey colour of the lines surrounding each black or white square. Your eye and brain can't help but see the lines as slanting, even when you know they are not.

Kanizsa triangle

Look at the white triangle in the middle of this image. In fact, there isn't one – there are no lines drawn. The three separate circles with a slice taken out of them are arranged in such a way that it's difficult not to see the triangle.

Moving spirals

This illusion is amazing. The effect of the patterns and the colours combine to create an illusion that the spirals are moving. If you look at the centre of one of the circles it will stop moving, but when you move your eyes to the next circle, the previous one will start to move again.

Blind spot

Your eyes can deceive you in a different way. Light is focused on a layer of special cells at the back of the eye to make a picture. But there's a gap in the special cells where the optic nerve enters each eye – this is your blind spot. You don't usually notice this gap because your brain fills in the missing information. Go to the website on page 89 to find your blind spot.

www.colourcube.com/illusions/illusion.htm

Magic and illusion

Magic tricks have been popular for thousands of years. One of the very first to be written about took place in Egypt 4,000 years ago: apparently, a magician called Dedi chopped off the heads of animals then magically replaced them. Either Dedi was a brilliant illusionist or he knew some very advanced surgical techniques.

David Copperfield's illusions are on a grand scale. He's made the Statue of Liberty disappear and walked through the Great Wall of China. In a surprising announcement in 2006, he claimed he had found the mythical fountain of youth on a Caribbean island. He says a pool of water seems to have life-giving properties, turning dead leaves green and reviving near-dead insects. Any updates on the miraculous fountain are eagerly awaited.

David Blaine, a modern-day magician and illusionist, is probably most famous for his strange, death-defying feats of endurance. He encased himself inside an ice-cube for 63 hours, and spent a week submerged in a water-filled sphere.

David Blaine appeared to levitate over the Grand Canyon. No one knows how he managed it.

Weird Thing To Do: Perform a Magic Trick

1 Lay out 20 cards as shown.

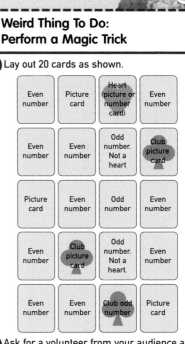

Even number	Picture card	Heart (picture or number card)	Even number
Even number	Even number	Odd number. Not a heart	Club picture card
Picture card	Even number	Odd number	Even number
Even number	Club picture card	Odd number. Not a heart.	Even number
Even number	Even number	Club odd number	Picture card

2 Ask for a volunteer from your audience and tell them to pick any card (without telling you which one it is).

3 Turn your back to your volunteer and cards. Tell them to move left or right to the nearest even number - if there are two the same distance away, they should choose one, and ignore any picture cards.

4 Now tell your volunteer to move up or down to the nearest club.

5 Now tell your volunteer to move left or right to the nearest odd number.

6 Now tell your volunteer to move up or down to the nearest heart.

7 Tell your volunteer that their card is the third card along the top row.

8 Take a bow.

www.kidzone.ws/magic

ECCENTRICS

Eccentrics are unconvential people who do things others find a little strange. In the past, some eccentrics were so strange that they became world famous!

Bear back riding

Jack Mytton was an eccentric English aristocrat, who was famous for being a daredevil. He kept a bear, which bit a chunk out of his leg (the bear refused to let Mytton ride it), he would rob his own guests while they were on their way home from visiting him, and he overturned carriages on a whim. He drank himself to death at an early age.

Battered mice and elephants' trunks

Frank Buckland was a Victorian eccentric who had an appetite for unusual dishes like rhinoceros pie, elephant's trunk soup, battered mice, giraffe. He even ate a panther that had been buried in a zoo (Buckland had it dug up and roasted). His father, William Buckland, was reported to have eaten the mummified heart of French King Louis XIV.

Rats for dinner

Susanna Kennedy, Countess of Eglintoune, was a strange lady who lived in the 18th century. The oddest thing about her was that she kept hundreds of pet rats, which had the run of her house, and often joined her for dinner: she would call them by tapping on a panel in the dining room.

Fart maniac

The famous French entertainer, Joseph Pujol, was known by most people as Le Petomane (French for 'fart maniac'). He entertained huge audiences at the end of the 19th century and beginning of the 20th century with his musical behind. He was the highest paid entertainer of his time.

www.historic-uk.com/CultureUK/briteccentrics.htm

21st century eccentrics

Eccentric people aren't just a thing of the past. They continue to surprise us with their unusual behaviour to this day.

More recent eccentrics include Graham Barker, the Australian who has collected his own navel fluff for more than 20 years and proudly displays it on his website.

Indian 'Snake Manu' eats earthworms – in 2003 he swallowed 200 in 30 seconds and won a world record. He also entertains himself by feeding live grass snakes up his nose and out through his mouth.

Monsieur Mangetout – French for "Mr Eat Everything" –regularly eats 900 g (32 oz) of metal per day, and his diet has included cutlery, shopping trolleys, razors, televisions, and even a light aircraft.

The Moleman
In 2006, a man in Hackney, East London, was banned from his home because he'd dug a network of tunnels underneath it. It had taken William Lyttle 40 years to remove 100 cubic m (3,500 cubic ft) of earth from underneath his house, creating tunnels more than 20 m (66 ft) long and up to eight metres (27 ft) deep.

Weird wedding
A Chinese man got married in 2007 in a ceremony with more than 100 guests. Liu Ye had a best man, and a bridesmaid, but no bride – he married a life-size foam cut-out of himself wearing a wedding dress. Liu Ye said the marriage was to 'express my dissatisfaction with reality'.

Eccentric entertainment

If you find weird things entertaining, you might like to go and see ...

KEN EDWARDS and his RATS

Be amazed as corageous Ken steps into a pair of tights filled with 47 live rats!

STEVIE STARR: THE REGURGITATOR

Gasp with wonder as Stevie swallows coins, lightbulbs, and even live creatures. He will regurgitate the objects in any order you desire - clean, dry and undamaged.

www.eccentricamerica.com

ESP

Extra Sensory Perception, or ESP, means sensing things without the use of the usual five senses – it's sometimes referred to as 'sixth sense'.

Examples of ESP include mind-reading, predicting the future, and moving objects without touching them. Many people believe in ESP. In fact, in a 2003 poll, nearly half of all British people claimed to have had personal experience of ESP. There's never been any conclusive evidence that it exists.

A famous series of experiments, called the 'ganzfeld test', seemed to provide evidence of ESP. In the experiments, a 'sender' tried to communicate a random image to another person in a different room, who was wearing headphones and a blindfold. The blindfolded person had to choose from one of four images.

You would expect them to guess the correct image one in four times – 25% of the time. The test was repeated more than 3,000 times and the actual success rate was 32%. The explanation for the extra 7% was given as ESP.

Later, the test was questioned and problems were found. The scientist conducting the experiments was accused of leading subjects towards the correct answer. An overwhelming majority of scientists are sceptical that ESP exists.

Uri Geller became famous for spoon-bending, mind-reading and making watches run fast, among other things. For more than 30 years he claimed his abilities were a result of ESP, but in 2007 he went back on his earlier claims and said he was just an entertainer. Various video recordings of Uri Geller performing appear to show him using tricks to achieve different effects.

The Million Dollar Challenge offers $1 million to anyone who can show proof of ESP.

Uri Geller claimed to be able to bend cutlery using only the power of his mind.

Mind reading

If you've ever seen a mind reader at work, you might wonder how on earth they do it. Are they really able to read minds?

Mind readers use a technique called 'cold reading'. This is a way of getting information from people without them even realising. Often this works well in large groups of people. They might start by asking the audience if anyone knows a man called David, for example, and take their lead from the people who respond positively. The idea is to begin with very general statements that could apply to anyone, such as, 'You are generally a kind and considerate person but can become very angry when pushed.' Then they look for reactions and make the statements more specific based on the way the person responds to the information.

With lots of practice and skill, mind-readers can produce amazing results. Some convince people that they have paranormal powers whereas others present their act as a trick, and even reveal some of their secrets.

Weird Thing To Do: Perform a Prediction Trick

To convince people you're a mind-reader, try this trick:

1. Before the act, look in a dictionary at page 108, write down the 9th entry on that page on a piece of paper and put it in a sealed envelope.

2. Ask for a volunteer and hand them the envelope. Hand the dictionary to someone else.

3. Ask the audience to call out three different numbers between 1 and 9. Write them down in plain view.

4. Ask your volunteer to reverse the three-digit number and take the bigger number away from the smaller one. (So if the number's 359, reverse it to get 953 and take 359 from it, to get 594.) If they're no good at sums, hand them a calculator.

5. Ask your volunteer to reverse the new number, then add the two together. (So in our example it would be 594 plus 495, making 1089.)

6. Ask the person with the dictionary to look at the first three digits of the number – 108 – and turn to that page. Ask them to count down to the ninth entry and read the word aloud. The volunteer with the envelope should then open the envelope and read aloud the word.

Take a bow.

This trick works because the number will always be 1089, no matter which three digits are called out. (It must be a three-digit number that can be reversed, so you must ask for three different numbers between 1 and 9 (232 wouldn't work, for example).

www.crystalinks.com/telepathy.html

Déjà vu

Have you ever had the eerie feeling that you've been somewhere, or experienced something before, even though you definitely haven't? That's the spooky phenomenon known as déjà vu, French for 'already seen'.

Even though it seems to be quite common, déjà vu is very difficult to study because, typically, the experience is over in a matter of seconds. It's never been fully explained, and there are all sorts of theories about it.

In 2007, scientists at the Massachusetts Institute of Technology identified specific receptors in the brain that control our ability to tell similar but different places and contexts apart. This might help to explain the sensation of déjà vu – your brain confuses a new place or experience with a remembered one.

One theory is that déjà vu can be explained by reincarnation (the body dies but the soul lives on to be reborn in a different body): people get the eerie feeling because they really have already had the experience, in a previous existence.

Another theory is that sometimes people are able to foretell the future in their dreams, although the dreams are forgotten. The feeling of déjà vu hapeens when the experience takes place in reality and the dream is remembered.

It could simply be that we experience déjà vu because we've seen something similar – perhaps in a film or a book if not in real life – and forgotten about it. The existence of the memory in the subconscious mind produces the sensation that something strange is happening.

Out-of-body experiences

Imagine hovering in the air, perhaps near the ceiling of your bedroom. Just as you're wondering how on earth you got up there, you look down and see ... yourself!

Many people have had the alarming experience of floating outside their body– though not all of them have been especially unsettled by it.

There are lots of reports of out-of-body experiences from people who have been clinically dead for seconds, or even minutes. Scientists think the answer might lie in a special part of the brain which, when stimulated in a particular way, may trigger an out-of-body experience. A lack of blood in the brain could also act as a trigger.

Some people say that they float around outside their bodies when they're in a dreamlike state. They say that this is definitely not a dream and that the experience is very different. Others attempt to trigger the experience deliberately: one method is meditation, and another is to remain on the edge of sleep without quite nodding off – people say that this creates a sort of trance which allows them to undergo an out-of-body experience.

Weird Thing To Do: Fool your Mind That Your Body Isn't Your Own

1. Set up two mirrors so that they face one another and reflect an infinite set of images.

2. Stand between the two mirrors and tilt your head so that you can only see your eyes in every other image. This will take a bit of fiddling about to achieve, but take the time to do it because the effect is worth it.

3. Stroke your cheek.

4. Aaaarggh! There's a stranger in front of you stroking their cheek!

It will only take a moment for you to realise that it is you and not a stranger. A neuroscientist called Eric Altschuler worked out this weird effect. Your brain is receiving confusing signals – in every other image you can't recognise your own face.

WEIRD BODY FACTS

The skin is the body's largest organ. If you laid out the skin of an average adult it would measure about 6 m2 (65 ft2). In just 1 cm2 (0.2 in2) of skin there are about 500 nerve cells, 40 sweat glands and 1 m (3.3 ft) of blood vessels. You shed skin all the time – house dust is mostly human skin.

It's impossible to lick your elbow – have a go, you know you want to.

Can you crack your knuckles? That sound isn't bones crunching but gas escaping from the joint. It'll take around half an hour before you can do it again because that's the time it takes for the gas to dissolve back into the fluid that surrounds the joint.

An adult human body has 206 bones. A child's has about 300 – the bones fuse together as you grow older.

There are up to 7 m (22 ft) of small intestine in the human body. The large intestine is wider than the small intestine, but it is only about 1.5 m (5 ft) long.

Most people have about 100,000 hairs on your head, but if you're a redhead you'll have fewer and if you're a blonde you might have as many as 140,000. Your hair grows up to 0.5 mm (0.02 in) in length every day and a single strand of it can tell scientists where you live, your ethnic origin and even your habits – though it doesn't reveal whether you're male or female.

The bones at the base of your spine are what's left of your tail. Our ancestors must have had tails – they're great for balance, but the need for it would have disappeared as humans began to walk upright. There are records of babies born with tails – an extended tailbone that doesn't cause any ill effects.

The appendix is a short tube attached to the large intestine. It has no function in humans – scientists believe it's left over from a plant-eating ancestor millions of years ago.

Did you know that if you're an average human being, your heart beats 100,000 times a day.

THE BRAIN

We've learned more about the human brain in the last 20 years than in the whole of the rest of history, yet it remains a mystery. The largest area of the brain, called the cerebral cortex, allows us to sense things, think and remember. It contains 15 billion brain cells, each of which make thousands of connections all the time. Studying these connections is very difficult, so we don't yet understand how they work.

The human brain weighs, on average, 2.25 kg (5 lb). It's already full size when you're about eight years old. Scientists don't yet know how much information the brain is capable of storing.

You probably have about 70,000 thoughts every day. Your brain produces more electrical impulses in one day than all the telecommunications systems in the world.

Different areas of the brain are highly specialised. One area deals with remembering names, and another with recognising faces.

Not surprisingly, the brain is the most protected organ in the human body. It has three layers of protection: the scalp, the skull and a membrane that covers the brain and spinal cord.

If you want to look at some real human brains, there's a brain museum in Peru with a collection of nearly 3,000. The world's biggest collection of brains is in the USA, at Harvard Brain Tissue Resource Center. They have nearly 6,700 brains.

The brain's surface, the cerebral cortex, stores most of the brain's information. It's wrinkled to fit inside the skull. If it were flattened out it would measure about 40 cm^2 (6 in^2) – that would need quite a big head!

Tattoos and piercings

People have been injecting indelible dye into their skins, and puncturing their bodies with jewellery, for thousands of years. The world's oldest mummy, a man who lived more than 5,000 years ago, has 57 tattoos on the skin of his back and legs, and he also has one of his ears pierced. Today, people all over the world have tattoos and piercings for religious reasons, to show status or membership, or because they like the way it looks.

Hole in one

Elaine Davidson holds the world record for the woman with the most piercings. In 2001, Guinness World Record officials counted her 720 piercings, many of them in her face. Now she has nearly 4,000 – and carries an extra 3 kg (7 lb) in weight because of them. There's also a world record for the most body piercings in one session: Kam Ma received more than 1,000 piercings in just under eight hours in 2006.

Tattoo record

New Zealander Lucky Diamond Rich is the most tattooed person in the world. Lucky's body is completely covered with ink, including the insides of his mouth and ears! So far he has spent more than 1,000 hours under a tattooist's needle. He also juggles chainsaws, swallows swords and rides a unicycle.

Food for thought

You can have just about anything you like tattooed on just about any part of your body. In 2007, one man had a full English breakfast tattooed on his head, complete with a knife and fork behind each ear. The same Welsh tattoo artist created a ham, cheese and pineapple pizza on another man's head a month later.

Weird medicine

Doctors are constantly baffled by strange medical conditions.
Some of them are so bizarre they might seem difficult to believe...

One case in the 1990s was completely unique: a 49-year-old woman had an epileptic fit whenever she heard the voice of Mary Hart, a US TV presenter. No one could understand why the woman had seizures when she heard Hart's voice. There have been no new cases of Mary Hart having this effect on other people.

Foreign Accent Syndrome isn't quite so rare: there have been 50 recorded cases. Sufferers are people who have had a stroke (a brain injury caused by an interruption of blood flow) or a traumatic injury to the head, and suddenly start speaking with a new accent. In 2006, a woman from near Newcastle, UK, found that her usual accent had been replaced with a different one after a stroke – it was described as Jamaican, Slovak and French Canadian. In 1999, a woman from Indiana, USA, began speaking with a British accent – a mixture of cockney and West Country – even though she had never been to Britain and didn't watch British TV shows.

Exploding Head Syndrome is a weird condition where sufferers experience an extremely loud noise inside their heads. It mostly happens during sleep and, though it isn't dangerous (your head doesn't actually explode), it is terrifying and distressing. So far, no one has found out why it happens.

There
have been
thousands of recorded
cases of Alien Hand Syndrome.
The patient's hand seems to have
a mind of its own, and operates
independently of the patient's wishes –
opening doors, writing, undoing
buttons or zips. In one case, the
hand tried to strangle its owner.
The strange phenomenon
occurs after brain surgery
or brain injury.

Dead and buried

There are roughly 6.5 billion human beings alive today. But at least ten times that number have lived and died in the 50,000 or so years of human history. What's happened to them? There are various ways of dealing with dead bodies, some of which might sound a bit weird...

Tree house

Tree burials have been practised in Siberia, North America, Australia and parts of Africa. They are still used in some places around the world. The dead person is wrapped in cloth or matting, placed high up in the branches of a tree, and left to decompose.

Bird feed

Followers of the Zoroastrian religion leave dead bodies high up in towers that are open to the sky, known as Towers of Silence. The bodies are left there to be picked at by birds of prey and bleached by the sun, for over a year. Then, finally, the bones are removed. Tibetan Sky Burial also provides food for birds, though it's not practised much any more: dead bodies are cut up and left on the mountainside for the vultures, so that all the dead person's remains leave the earth. In fact, sometimes the remains are mixed with other food to make them more appetising for the birds.

Deep freeze

Cryonic science is being researched, developed, and practised today, and it could give people the possibility of a second life. Dead bodies are stored at extremely low temperatures soon after they have been pronounced dead. The hope is that, one day, medical science will have advanced enough to cure whatever disease killed them in the first place. Although medicine is advancing rapidly, the freezing process damages human cells, so the frozen bodies may have a very long time to wait. There are two institutions in the US that carry out cryonics – between them they have about 150 frozen bodies in deep freeze.

Deadly diamonds

A US company is the first to offer to turn your dead relative into a synthetic diamond. Carbon is extracted from cremated remains, then made into a diamond using intense pressure and high temperatures. Up to 100 diamonds can be made from one dead body.

http://science.howstuffworks.com/cryonics.htm

Weird games

Knock-out chess

One of the world's most bizarre games is an unlikely combination of chess and boxing – yes, the game of cunning strategy really is combined with the sport where people punch one another wearing giant gloves.

Since 2003, when the first competition was held, chessboxing has become popular all over the world, especially in Russia and the Ukraine. Players alternate four-minute chess rounds with three-minute boxing rounds. You might think that someone who was big and burly and good at boxing would have an unfair advantage – and you'd be right. However, all competitors have to reach a minimum standard of chess before they're allowed into the boxing ring!

Dwyle flonking

Some odd games are played in English pubs and one of the strangest is the little-known game of dwyle flonking.

It's an outdoor game for two large teams: one of the teams forms a circle around a member of the opposing team (the 'flonker'), who holds a broom handle (the 'driveller') with a beer-soaked rag (the 'dwyle') on top of it. Using the driveller, the flonker tries to fling the dwyle onto a member of the other team, with points being awarded depending which part of the body is hit!

The world dry foam flinging championships are held every year in England.

Strange sport

Going to extremes

'Extreme ironing' is an unusual sport, where competitors do something dangerous and exciting, such as climbing mountains or caving, and iron clothes at the same time. Based on the same idea, 'extreme accounting' sees suited number-crunchers scuba diving, skiing, pot-holing, abseiling or even water-skiing while accounting. The world champion is Keet Van Zyl, a South African chartered management accountant.

Bog snorkelling

Bog-snorkellers are more common than you might expect. Every year since 1985, world championships have been held in Wales. Competitors snorkel through a 60 m (200 ft) trench dug in a peat bog in the fastest possible time. Other sports popular with bog-snorkellers are Mountain Bike bog snorkelling and Underwater Hockey!

Wife carrying

'Wife carrying' began as a Finnish joke but now attracts competitors from all over the world. Male competitors race with female teammates over their shoulders or on their backs over a 250 m (820 ft) course, which includes water obstacles and hurdles. Major competitions are held in Sonkajarvi, Finland, and Wisconsin and Michigan, USA.

More weird sport...

Mountain unicycling – just like mountain biking but with fewer wheels.

Zorbing – rolling down a hill inside a giant inflatable ball.

Elephant polo – like the kind played on horseback, but wth much longer sticks.

Mud pit pillow-fighting – competitors are suspended above a mud pit as they bash each other with feather pillows at the annual pillow-fighting world championships held in California.

Weird festivals

Are you interested in giant cheese rolling, shouting very loudly or naked wrestling? If so, make a note of the following dates in your diary...

Randwick Cheese Festival

Date: May
Place: Randwick, Gloucestershire, England

On the first Sunday of May, three cheeses are rolled anticlockwise around the church, then one of them is cut up and eaten by the villagers. The next Saturday there's a procession through the town of villagers dressed as Tudors, led by a man waving a wet mop. The Mayor is dunked in a special pool, then the procession continues to a steep slope and two cheeses are rolled down it. Other British cheese-rolling festivals take the form of races, like the one in Chester that takes place every February.

The cheese-rolling race in Chester

National Hollerin' Contest

Date: Every June
Place: Spivey's Corner, North Carolina, USA

Thousands gather to take part in a contest to see who can shout loudest. There are separate events for men, women, teens and juniors.

Oil Wrestling Festival

Date: First week in September
Place: Elmali, Turkey

For centuries, Burly young men gather in the small mountain town of Elmali to take part in the covetted oil wrestling championship!

Baby-jumping Festival

Date: First Sunday after Catholic feast day of Corpus Christi
Place: Castrillo de Murcia, Spain

Men dressed as the devil, carrying whips or truncheons, leap over defenceless babies – an event known as El Colacho. The organisers of the festival rush about chasing and generally terrorising everyone.

www.oddee.com/item_96372.aspx

More weird festivals

Air Guitar World Championships

Date: September
Place: Oulu, Finland

Since 1996, air guitarists from all over the world have been competing at Oulu. In the first round, competitors are given a classic guitar tune to follow by the judges. In the second round they can choose their own.

Naga Fireballs Festival

Date: First full moon in October
Place: Mekong River, Nong Khai, Thailand

The strange phenomenon of the Naga fireballs is often seen in October, and sometimes in other months too. Glowing, reddish balls rise from the river before disappearing. No one knows how or why it happens. One explanation is that they are caused by flammable natural gases; another is that they come from the Naga, a supernatural serpent. A festival is held Every October to celebrate the strange lights.

Midnight Wrestling

Date: February
Place: Saidaiji Temple, Japan

Thousands of men dressed ONLY in loincloths gather in the Saidaiji Temple in an unusual tradition dating back to the 1500s. The men run around the temple, then WRESTLE with one another until, at midnight, a pair of wands are thrown by priests into the crowd and the men scramble for them. The two that are SUCCESFUL are rewarded with a LUCKY year ahead.

Songkran is a festival in Thailand which involves people throwing water at one another for three days.

EGG BASHING

Date: Easter Sunday
Place: Berne, Switzerland

On Easter Sunday, people bring decorated eggs to a square in the centre of Berne, where they SMASH them to bits in an egg-bashing competition, rather like a conker fight (but with eggs, obviously).

Woolly Worm Festival

Date: October
Place: Banner Elk, North Carolina, USA

Woolly Bear Caterpillars, also known as Woolly Worms, are raced up a string. Around 1,000 caterpillars take part, and the winner is known as the 'weather worm' – the stripes on its body are supposed to predict the weather for the coming winter.

Dowsing

Dowsers are people who detect buried water, metal, oil or even people, by means that remained unexplained. The process of dowsing is most commonly used to find water, and it's sometimes known as 'water divining' or 'water witching'. It's still widely practised today.

Some dowsers use Y-shaped twigs.

Most dowsers use a dowsing stick, which might be a Y-shaped twig, or sometimes a metal rod or two straight wooden sticks. The stick, or sticks, move when the dowser is above water – they might twitch downwards, or cross if the dowser is using two.

There are different theories about why the rods move: some believe it's due to magnetic forces or other geological forces, whilst others believe in electrical currents, or the dowser's extraordinary sensitivity to water. It's also possible that dowsers watch out for natural signs – greener grass, or dips in the landscape – without being conscious of doing so.

Some people believe that the rods move because of the dowser's involuntary muscle movements, and the results are no more than luck. Others believe that dowsers find water by paranormal means.

There have been various dowsing experiments, using water buried in plastic pipes or bottles. None of them has proved the dowsers to be any more successful than you'd expect from luck.

Weird Thing To Do: Dowse for Water

Why not set up your own dowsing experiment?

You need: 10-20 cardboard boxes or buckets, the same number of bottles, friends with dowsing rods – they can use a twig or a coat hanger. The greater the number of friends, the more significant your results will be.

1. Fill half the bottles with water and leave the others empty.

2. Place each bottle underneath a box or bucket spaced at regular intervals (it is a good idea to do this outside).

3. Ask each friend to walk the course with a dowsing rod. Paying careful attention to their dowsing rod, they must tell you which boxes/buckets contain water and which don't. Record the answers.

4. Analyse your results. Do any of your friends seem to have special powers?

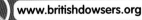

www.britishdowsers.org

Weird art

If anyone ever tells you that modern art is poo, you can reply that some of it is, quite literally. One of the weirdest pieces of art of the 20th century is by Italian artist Piero Manzoni. It consists of labelled cans of his own poo. Unfortunately, since they were created in the 1960s, some of the cans have exploded because of expanding gases. In 2002, the Tate Gallery in London bought one of Manzoni's cans of poo for more than £22,000.

Some art is also rubbish: artist Justin Gignac goes around New York City collecting rubbish, which he then places in clear plastic cubes, signs, dates and sells as works of art. At Tate Britain in London, a cleaner removed a bag of rubbish and put it in a crusher, only to discover that it was part of an art installation by artist Gustav Metzger. An art storage company mistook a work of art by Anish Kapoor for rubbish and threw it away – then had to pay out £350,000 in compensation.

In 2004, American artist Emily Duffy made a 1.5-m- (5-ft-) tall, 800 kg (1800 lbs) sculpture from more than 18,000 bras, rolled up together like a ball of wool. Cheryl Capezzuti, another American artist, makes her sculptures entirely out of lint found inside tumble dryers. Artist Stan Murmur doesn't need brushes to create his paintings of flowers – he uses his paint-covered bottom.

Museum of Weird

Some people have interesting collections of antiques or art. Other collections are stranger – and can include anything from toilets to garden gnomes...

Museum of Mud

It seems that, somewhere in the world, there's a collection of just about anything you can name, no matter how odd. The Museum of Dirt in Boston is a collection of soil from all over the world. There's even a museum of umbrella covers in Peake's Island, Maine.

Public convenience

A museum in Kiev, Ukraine, is dedicated to the history of the toilet, from a primitive hole in the ground to the latest in cutting-edge toilet technology. After an unfortunate incident soon after it was opened in 2007, the museum had to add 'Not for Use' signs to all of its exhibits. There's also an 'International Museum of Toilets' in New Delhi, India.

Hair lair

In Avanos, Turkey, there are more than 16,000 samples of women's hair on display. Another human hair museum, in Missouri, USA, exhibits hair that has been made into jewelllery and decorative wreaths, much of it more than 100 years old.

Parasites

The Meguro Parasitological Museum, in Tokyo, Japan, displays nothing but case after case of parasites (creatures that live off other creatures) and gruesome examples of what they can do to their hosts. Possibly the most horrible exhibit is an 8.8-m- (28-ft-) long tape worm, which was removed from a man's stomach.

Ham and Spam

The hamburger museum in Florida, USA, contains over a thousand hamburger-related objects, including a burger-shaped waterbed and a motorbike. It's the world's only hamburger museum, though there are are others dedicated to different types of food... If you've ever tried Spam (a ham-based processed meat product) you might be surprised to learn that there's a Museum of Spam in Austin, Minnesota, its American birthplace.

www.travelouk.com/features/weird-stuff.htm

BIZARRE BUILDINGS

**Some buildings are a little bit different from the ordinary –
some are strangely shaped and others use highly unusual
building materials.**

Chickens, ducks and UFOs

All sorts of unlikely buildings have been built as promotional aids for
businesses, like the KFC Big Chicken in Georgia, USA, which serves as
a landmark for road users and plane pilots. Other bizarre buildings
include a UFO-shaped bus station in Poland, a shop in New York, USA
which is shaped like a giant duck, and a teapot-shaped service station
in Washington, USA.

Bony building

In Sedlec, Czech Republic, stands one of the world's strangest
buildings. It's a Christian chapel with some very unusual interior
decoration: tens of thousands of human bones. The altar is made of
bones, there's a huge bone coat of arms, and a chandelier that uses all
206 bones in the human body at least once. The bones are the remains
of approximately 40,000 people who were buried in the graveyard but
moved to make way for more burials in the 1500s. They were then
arranged as they are today towards the end of the 19th century.

Shark attack

There's a surprise waiting for you in an ordinary suburban street in
Headington, Oxford, UK: a 7.5-m- (25-ft-) long fibreglass shark,
weighing 200 kg (450 lb), embedded head-first in the roof of an
otherwise normal terraced house. It first appeared in 1986. Oxford
City Council tried to have it removed but, after a legal battle lasting
many years, the shark was allowed to remain. Now local residents
are used to it.

Keep an eye out for water towers in the shape of various different objects, including a corn cob and an enormous bottles of tomato ketchup (both of which are in the USA).

Do you carelessly walk under ladders on Friday 13th? Do you carry a lucky rabbit's foot? Or do you take great care when handling mirrors? Whether you are superstitious or not, there are an awful lot of strange superstitions around.

Unlucky for some

In Western cultures the number 13 is often seen as unlucky. Most high-rise buildings don't have a 13th floor and some airports skip Gate 13.

In China, Japan, Korea and Hawaii the unlucky number is 4, and it's often skipped over in the same way. In some countries, it's not uncommon to find a high-rise building with no floor or room number 4, 13 or 14. In Korea, odd numbers are considered lucky and even numbers unlucky – though they tend to use all of them anyway as it would be a bit confusing otherwise!

SUPERSTITIONS

Some strange superstitions:

★ If a pregnant woman puts two spoons in her saucer she'll have ginger twins.

★ Eating stolen bacon is a cure for constipation.

★ Never cut your toenails after dark: the cuttings will form into an evil spirit.

★ It's lucky to put your underpants on back to front.

A stroke of luck

Depending on where you live, black cats are either good luck or bad luck, especially if they cross your path. Generally, they're seen as good luck in Ireland but another Irish superstition says that if you run over a cat it's 17 years of bad luck.

In France, cats are said to lead to buried treasure. But in some places our feline friends are seen as evil eavesdroppers: in Holland superstitious people actually shut them out of the room if they're having a private conversation. Apparently it's bad luck to cross a stream carrying a cat. But perhaps the strangest cat superstition of all is to give a cat its food in your left shoe a week before your wedding to bring good luck.

Fear of the number 13 has its own word: triskaidekaphobia.

Odd jobs

One of the strangest jobs of all time was that of Royal Farter. Henry II's Farter, Roland Le Pettour, did such a good job of whistling, leaping about and guffing that the King rewarded him with an entire estate in Suffolk.

But there are still plenty of weird jobs about today...

WANTED
Fantasy Broker

Duties: Making dreams come true.

If you want to ride an elephant, sky-dive naked or drive a monster truck across Europe, you might want to employ the services of a Fantasy Broker, who'll sort out the whole thing... for a large fee. There are several fantasy firms in existence.

WANTED
Sewer Diver

Duties: Diving into sewers and removing blockages.

Sewer divers are employed in large sewers all over the world. In Mexico City, for example, a city of more than 19 million people, the sewers are overworked and often blocked. A team of sewer divers is employed to dive in bacteria-laden sewage to locate and remove blockages. Whatever the divers are paid, it's not enough.

WANTED
Odour judger

Duties: Sniffing armpits

Odour judgers are paid to work out the effectiveness (or otherwise) of deodorants – by smelling people's armpits. Odour judgers are also used for testing mouthwash and toothpaste.

WANTED

Egg smeller

Duties: Sniffing broken eggs.

Egg smellers are trained to test eggs that are used in processed foods to make sure the eggs aren't spoiled.

Weird crimes

Ghostly burglar

In 1974, a ghost was believed to have set off a burglar alarm in a house in Norfolk. Nothing was missing but footprints on the floor, made by a single shoe, stopped at a brick wall. The house was believed to be haunted by the ghost of a one-legged priest.

Stolen bridges

Strangely enough, there have been cases of stolen bridges throughout many different parts of the world. In 2008, thieves in Russia managed to nick a 200-tonne bridge without anyone noticing and two other Russian bridge thefts took place in 2007. An outbreak of bridge theft took place in the Northern Territory of Australia in 2004 – 11 were stolen, the longest 20 m (66 ft) long.

Strangely stupid

In 2004, a Romanian man stole a car and crashed into a tree after less than a kilometer – he was lucky to have got that far, since he is blind. Another man stole a small aircraft from an airport in Texas despite the fact that he didn't know how to fly a plane – he quickly crashed into electricity lines but was unhurt and walked home, where he was arrested.

Pants!

A Norwegian man robbed a bank masked in his own underpants. He hadn't realized however that his wife's name was on the reverse of the paper he handed to the bank cashier and he was soon arrested. The man said he'd been so drunk that he didn't remember robbing a bank, though he had become suspicious the next day when he found a huge wad of cash in his pocket and saw the newspaper photograph of the robber wearing a pair of his pants.

CANNIBALISM

We get the word 'cannibalism' from the Carib or Canib people of the West Indies, all of whom were wiped out by the Europeans who arrived from the end of the 15th century. The Caribs had a horrible reputation for eating human flesh, but it's probably not true: the invading Europeans wanted an excuse for enslaving the native people.

Cannibals have existed throughout human history. There's evidence to suggest the Neanderthals ate bits of one another, and so did prehistoric human beings. In some isolated places in the South Pacific, people were still eating one another in the 19th century. The Reverend Thomas Baker, found this out when he was in a remote Fijian village – he made the mistake of touching the chief's head, and was immediately killed, cooked and eaten. In 2003, descendants of the cannibalistic villagers held a special ceremony to make a formal apology to the descendants of the Reverend Baker.

Today, members of the Korawai tribe in Indonesia are believed to eat human flesh.

Sometimes people eat other people quite by accident. In 2008, a piece of human tongue was served in a hospital canteen in Slovenia – a doctor spotted an unusual piece of meat in his chicken risotto and sent it for tests.

Weird food

What you consider to be weird food depends on where you live: some people love eating raw fish, while others have locusts for lunch. See what you think of these...

Shark snack

Hakarl is an Icelandic national dish. It's made by gutting a basking shark and burying it in gravel for about three months, then hanging up the flesh to dry for a few more months. The meat of the shark can't be eaten unless it's processed in this way because it's poisonous. Even when it has been buried, dried and finally served in cubes it smells of cleaning fluid and most people gag involuntarily when they first try it.

Fatal fish

Would you eat a fish that could be fatally poisonous? Plenty of people eat pufferfish, which contain deadly amounts of the poison tetradoxin (the same one found in box jellyfish). In Japan, where it's known as fugu, the most prized variety is also the most poisonous. Fugu chefs train for three years before they're let loose in a restaurant. Even so, several people die every year from puffer fish that haven't been prepared correctly – there's no antidote and the victim remains fully conscious, though completely paralysed, until death.

A lovely cuppa

The world's most expensive coffee is luak coffee, which costs around US $150 per kilo. It's so special because it has to be hand-picked from the poo of a civet cat called a luak. The luak, a creature a bit like a weasel and native to Indonesia, eats the fruit that surround coffee beans. The animal excretes the partly digested beans, then people fish the beans out of the luak's poo. Apparently the animal's digestive system makes the coffee worth every penny.

British chef Heston Blumenthal creates unusual dishes, including snail porridge and egg-and-bacon ice cream.

www.simnet.is/gullis/jo/shark.htm

Insect eaters

If you think eating insects is strange, you're in the minority: it's only really in Europe and North America that eating insects is considered weird. There are at least 1,400 species of edible insect and many people relish the taste: various grubs, grasshoppers, ants and other insects are commonly on the menu in Africa, South America, Asia and Australia.

A Mexican restaurant in Dresden, Germany, began to include maggots on the menu in 2007. The maggots, imported from Mexico, feature in salads, cocktails and even ice cream, or are eaten fried with cactus and corn. The maggot menu has proved a great success, so maybe bugs will start becoming popular in Europe too.

Maggot cheese

A far less sensible creepy-crawly snack is 'maggot cheese'. Even though it's been banned by the government, it's still eaten in Sardinia. It's cheese, made from sheep's milk, that's been left outside in the sun, where flies land on it and lay their eggs. When the maggots hatch, apparently the maggotty cheese is delicious on toast.

You're already eating insects, whether you know it or not: just about everything we eat has minute bits of bugs in it, and there are even government regulations on the subject.

Weird Thing To Do: Make a Chocolate Insect Snack

Insects are full of protein but low in fat and taste delicious. Why not try this recipe – you'll need to find somewhere that sells crickets, and the insects should be cleaned and, preferably, dead first. You'll also need your favourite chocolate – milk or plain – and some wax paper.

1. Bake crickets at 180 degrees C (350 degrees F, gas mark 4) for 20 minutes or until crunchy.

2. Melt the chocolate by breaking it into squares and putting it in a heat-proof basin over a saucepan of simmering water. Stir it all the time, otherwise it'll go lumpy.

3. Dip your crickets in the chocolate then leave them to dry on wax paper.

4. Feast upon your weird chocolate snack.

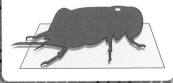

Air guitar – miming playing the guitar to music.

Antibiotics – substances that kill or inhibit the growth of bacteria.

Bacteria – tiny organisms, living in bodies, organic matter, water or soil, that often cause disease.

Biodynamics – a type of organic farming that uses the various phases of the Moon for guidance; for example, different crops will be planted during different phases.

Blind spot – an area within your field of vision that you are unable to see.

Cannibals – humans who eat other humans.

Carnivorous plants – plants that survive by eating meat (such as insects).

Cephalopod family – a class of molluscs, including the octopus and the squid, that have tentacles around the head.

Coincidences – when more than one similar event happens at the same time or in the same place, without the events seeming to be linked.

Contagious – catching, infectious.

Cryonics – when dead bodies are stored at extremely low temperatures, in the hope that one day they can be revived.

Disembowelling – removing the bowels of a person or animal. Electrons – negatively charged particles.

Germination – beginning to grow.

Infrasound – sound frequencies below the range of human hearing, some of which can make people and animals feel uneasy and anxious.

Meteorites – large lumps of rock that fall from space to Earth.

Meteor showers – shooting stars (small particles that become visible as a streak of light when they fall from space and hit the Earth's atmosphere).

Milligram – a thousandth of a gram.

Optical illusion – an image that tricks your brain into thinking you're seeing something you're not.

Organism – a biological being (such as an animal).

Paranormal – not explained by science.

Regurgitate – bringing up something you've eaten, from the stomach to the mouth.

Superstition – an irrational belief that something can bring good or bad luck.

Tentacles – long, protruding, flexible parts of creatures such as jellyfish.

Toxic – poisonous.

Voodoo – a religion originating from Africa; people communicate through trances, dreams and rituals, and use spells or curses.

The publishers would like to thank the following for their kind permission to reproduce their photographs:

1 Maximilian Weinzierl / Alamy; 2-3 Image Source / Rex Features; Design Pics Inc. / Alamy; 4-5 PATRICK BARTH / Rex Features; 6-7 Nature Picture Library / Rex Features; 8-9 M Marschall / Newspix / Rex Features; 10-11 Pacific Stock / Fleetham Dave / Photolibrary; 12-13 Rick & Nora Bowers / Alamy; 14-15 Goss Images / Alamy; 16-17 Adrian Sherratt / Alamy; 18-19 PHOTOTAKE Inc. / Alamy; 20-21 Design Pics Inc. / Alamy; 22-23 AGB Photo Library / Rex Features; 24-25 OSF / David M Dennis / Photolibrary; 26-27 Bob Elsdale / Photonica / Getty Images; 28-29 Mary Evans Picture Library / Alamy; 30-31 OSF / Enrique Aguirre / Photolibrary; 32-33 Olivier Grunewald / OSF / Photolibrary; 34-35 Photodisc / Alamy; 36-37 nagelestock.com / Alamy; 38-39 Dale O'Dell / Alamy; 40-41 Kevin Schafer / Alamy; 42-43 Imagesate RM / The Print Collector / Photolibrary; 44-45 The Travel Library / Rex Features; 46-47 andy rouse – wildlife / Alamy; 48-49 OSF / MIchael Fogden / Photolibrary; 50-51 Dale O'Dell / Alamy; 52-53 creative stock images / Alamy; 54-55 Robert Estall photo agency / Alamy; 56-57 Mary Evans Picture Library / Alamy; 58-59 Swim Ink2, LLC / Corbis; 60-61 Christopher Cormack / Corbis; 62-63 Dale O'Dell / Alamy; 64-65 Sherman Hines / Alamy; 66-67 Beinecke Rare Book and Manuscript Library, Yale University; 68-69 istockphoto; 70-71 iStockphoto; 72-73 Manor Photography / Alamy; 74-75 Nonstock / ECHOS / Photolibrary; 76-77 iStockphoto; 78-79 blickwinkel / Alamy; 80-81 JUPITERIMAGES / PIXLAND / Alamy; 82-83 PATRICK BARTH / Rex Features; 84-85 SHIZUO KAMBAYASHI / AP / PA Photos; 86-87 photazz / Shutterstock; 88-89 photazz / Shutterstock; 90-91 NetaDegany/iStockphoto; 92-93 Mary Evans Picture Library / Alamy;

94-95 OSF / John Downer / Photolibrary; 96-97 Image Source / Rex Features; 98-99 FRANK BELL / Rex Features; 100-101 Stephen Coburn / Shutterstock; 102-103 Caro / Alamy; 104-105 blickwinkel / Alamy; 106-7 London Scientific Films / OSF / photolibrary; 108-109 Alistair Berg / Alamy; 110-111 graficart.net / Alamy; 112-113 Image Source / Rex Features; 114-115 Hypermania / Alamy; 116-117 Phil Rees / Rex Features; 118-119 South West News Service / Rex Features; 120-121 Sipa Press / Rex Features; 122-123 John Glover / Alamy; 124-125 Andrew Caballero Reynolds / Alamy; 126-127 Apex News and Pictures Agency / Alamy; 128-129 Nora Pelyi / Rex Features; 130-131 artpartner-images.com / Alamy; 132-133 Alan Wesley / Shutterstock; 134-135 Sean Gladwell / Alamy; 136-137 Frank Chmura / Alamy; 138-139 David Fleetham / Alamy; 140-141 Stefan Mokrzecki / Photolibrary; 144 Nature Picture Library / Rex Features.